Dreams of the Caucasus

Also by Norman Jope

For the Wedding-Guest (Stride, 1997)
The Book of Bells and Candles (Waterloo, 2009)
Aphinar (Waterloo, forthcoming)

Dreams of the Caucasus

Norman Jope

Shearsman Books
2010

First published in the United Kingdom in 2010 by
Shearsman Books Ltd
58 Velwell Road
Exeter EX4 4LD

www.shearsman.com

ISBN 978-1-84861-129-0
First Edition

Acknowledgements
Some of these works, or earlier versions of them, have appeared in the
magazines *JAAM* (New Zealand), *Poetry NZ* (New Zealand)*, Poetry
Salzburg Review* (Austria), *Sentence* (USA), *Shearsman*, *Tears in the Fence*
and *Tremblestone* and on the websites *Eyewear*, *Great Works*,
NthPosition and *Stride*.

The author would like to thank Lynda for her companionship, from near
and not-so-far, and all those involved in the Language Club (Plymouth)—
particularly Tim Allen, Kenny Knight, Philip Kuhn and Steve Spence—for
their fellowship and support whilst these pieces were being written. Thanks
are also due to Brian Clements, Rupert Loydell, David Miller, Roderick
Muncey and Nikki Santilli for their encouragement; and to the musicians
Jon Hassell, Brian Eno, Geir Jenssen/Biosphere and Toru Takemitsu for
helping to inspire the sequences 'Suspended Gold' (Hassell/Eno) and
'Blue Skin' (Jenssen/Takemitsu).

CONTENTS

VII. *from* **Departures** (2008–2009)

I

Suspended Gold

Erg

Soft sand covers the shoes and scratches the lenses of the eyes. The sand is the colour of a filtered lens, that is trained on a blank surface. Where does that colour come from? It hovers and drifts as the shadows darken and harden, ambassadors of an ethereal weight. Ergs extend in a limitless expanse, forming waves and crescents of golden dust, on a horizon of suspended gold.

The erg's imperative is the silence of the footprint, which can outlast one's life. Traces in the erg—the hyena, the jackal, the gazelle, the horse. The mark of the eye of the bird of the night, left in the space at the bottom of the slope, insinuates that the vultures are circling. Addax and oryx skip across the dunes on delicate hooves, filling their jowls with *aristida plumose*. Here is the lazily-shrivelled fire-meat of the interior.

The void of the eye fills up with sand, on the skin of a world just 93 million miles away from the source of its conflagrations. It is possible to stand, tongue roofing the mouth, in the face of a blast that sends all water heavenward, causing the lips to crack and the tongue to swell. Facing the seas ahead, the sable seas which would scorch the naked feet, it is possible to inscribe the Poem of the Clearing but, in this unforested place without abundant wells, the text becomes a series of glances. It exists in an eye that has become more brittle than stone, that is on the verge of becoming powder where the Many confronts the One.

So silence confronts Silence, the eye confronts the Eye . . . the body of the sand confronts the body of the sky which darkens, daily, to reveal the stars that also gather into dunes, that deposit their silver, gold and silence over the backdrop, covering the shoes with which we walk from the other side, scratching the lenses that we use, when walking there, to observe our shadows walking.

Serir

And then there is *serir*. A cleansed space, a location wind whistles through, arranging the remains. A somewhere else, where nothing prevails and the horizons are constant.

We can only define it by moving slowly. There are no nests for the arrows that fall.

This is a space where silence enters the pilgrim—enshrines the one who renounces action and event. A surface of refusal reaches into the refusal that is death, a domain where every gobbet of flesh is razored directly from bone.

Its tenuous gravel is arranged on pallid sand, beneath a sky in which nothing, not even the human eye, is tangible. Its expanses erode all primate curiosity, returning the mind to reptilian languor. The brain is spring-cleaned, as if by an injection of menthol.

Each stone here is a *ka'aba*, the tiny temple of a posthumous grace, on which a black sweat drips from marmoreal bones. They turn to gold, then scarlet, in the light that dismantles them.

Coming here means to assent to a deeper nakedness, in which all flesh is superfluous. A heap of bones at the bottom of the star-well, one is filleted by photonic vultures.

Knowledge, here, is scorched. Belief, ignited.

We are suddenly here, where the music stops, and the invention of the Names of God begins.

L'arbre du Téneré

The mobile rattles in red wind, a jewel-boned scarecrow whose existence nails the past to a shadow thrown brokenly on gravel, purloined by the lizard playing dead in a limitless noon.

The tree that it supplants was plucked for posterity by a Libyan trucker— outlasting his liver-faced embarrassment, it was carried off and tapped for Carbon-14 in the Musée de Niamey. It could have been the product of a seed dropped from the arse of a passing vulture, catching by chance the merest sparkle of fetched water from the well nearby. Yet it grew to become a landmark, the only tree discovered in a region the size of France . . . a Michelin symbol placed on the small-scale map for years after its destruction.

So what would it mean to lie there now . . . cooled by its non-existent shadow at the height of day, or in the sulphuric-acid sharpness of night's immensities, so that a tiny portion of the geode-encrusted sky was obscured by the flaps of its desperate moisture?

The Japanese artist's monument blinks in the solar glare, but the absent tree, the one that was stunned and kidnapped, the one that is dead yet privileged, puts forth its shade and the *azalais* halt to take a reading from its non-existence. Unbending in absence, resplendent integer of zero's One, it locates what is most remote, and directs it into the bull's eye of the earth.

Les nuits de Bilma

There are salt-clay bricks under flat roofs seldom rained on, flaking in laser sun. A street filled with sand, which rises towards a fort. An abandoned pool, half-filled. Evenings, sweating by a paraffin lamp.

But, at night, the sky is filled with crystals of salt—so many, that the sand seems rivalled. Orion guards the passage across the Ténéré. Cassiopeia writhes at the zenith—Polaris lights the road the colonists took. The sound of pestles fades in the static-laden air.

No breeze, no cloud. To be out there, standing by the wells, away from the stacks of moulded salt, the yoghurt-coloured crater-lakes where the brine has settled. To be out there, licking the stars with all the eyes one has.

On a night like this, the earth's protective veils fall away. What is left is exposure, not so much chilling the spine as filling it with a golden sap, so that the body becomes a fountain of leaves in love with the outer darknesses, the magnetic onslaughts from the war chests of other stars than the implacable sun.

Pinned to the narrow crevasse of a single night, where both one's birth and one's death advance like walls of salt-clay cast into utter shadow, there is only one direction that can be scouted with a calm heart. So look up, to the skies of Bilma—feel the planet tighten under the feet, drink in the absinthes of abandonment, never so alive as when so lost, not needing shade of any description.

Atakor

Forced upwards—basalt, phonolite, andesite, trachite.

Denuded, so that the pipes remain and only the pipes, in the form of cones and dog-toothed plugs that rise above the surrounding plain. Black spires of rock, like the spars of enormous ships, or the pinnacles of Breton churches—solid yet brittle, forced upwards into the sky flesh, prickly as doum-palm barbs on naked feet.

This is a porcupine of a landscape—defending itself, in vain, against the erosive forces that assail it, to the point where there is no longer anything intact that can, with meaning, be defended, so that the gesture is mechanical, the charm-spell of a weary old man who knows that the ravens are already picking the locks of his eyes but is nonetheless trying, as if still young, to shoo them away. He is spare and defaced, yet continues to wave at the heavens as the skin on his back turns to chitin.

To be here means to share in its dissolution and, no less, its jagged defiance. One travels exposed yet upright, forced from the womb towards the sun, denuded by that very sun which turns each item of clothing to a scar—a human column, destined to fall yet holding one's ground. Not even a tower of breath, for breath begins to thin in the tamarisk-scented upland air—but solid despite one's brittleness, an agent of geometry resisting the temptations of erosion, the ultimate sleep that is the risk of the *serir*.

Reg

The gravel coats the eye. The sun is a bowl of acid, drawing the softer colours out of the face. Each mile is ripped from the silence. The stars melt in their cages, as a heap of dust explodes and covers the moon with the spectre of itself. Everything swims before the mouth.

There is *nothing* here. Perhaps it could be mined, the perfect excuse for speculation. It is smooth, hard, razor-finned and brutally contemporary. It exhausts all signatories, sealing the lips of the herald. On a shield of granite, schist and gneiss, it loiters and squats. It wipes the distant sound of pestles, that hammer millet in oases to the south.

Azure on gold—heraldic noon. Brilliance is raised to the status of fire. The gravel dismantles the eye.

One must wait for the stars, which reappear cooled in the rapidly freezing skies of evening. Then the world swings open, devouring all models of itself, all compromised measures.

Lost on the *reg*, having walked a plank of words into its gold-grey sea, one imagines that tomorrow's landscape is pre-ordained, that the ultimate nothing stretches across the pupil of the eye. But then something changes, if only for a moment—and, beyond the pollens of dream, the horizon blows open, revealing a presence that spins webs across the shallow gulf between nothing and something, enabling a weightless moment to assert itself. Elusive as a *waran*, flicking its tail in the furnace of another day.

Navigation: The Seven Daughters of the Night

Waking chilled, in the hours before dawn, one encounters the Daughters. They rise, like larks, in the late summer sky.

Their sapphire tinge is strong, as piquant as mint. Near them, the Cyclopean eye of Aldebaran is ox-blood red, a haemorrhage of light against its obsidian backdrop.

Beneath these stars, the form of the Hunter scintillates—his belt is a series of ivory studs, his sword a misty flash of alien metal. Even the star-names of Orion resonate with a language of the desert—as if, wherever seen on earth, their most appropriate sky were here. The desert, like the sea, remains in love with its stars.

The Daughters rise at the coldest point of the night, when—even at this time of year—the stones are already sheathed in lattices of hoarfrost. These icy mistresses of absence refuse the nights of sweat which seek them to the south, retreating behind cloud. Imperious as they are glacial, they turn to face a place that is more lethal, by far, than any earthly desert— and yet, they connect to the deserts of earth as if they were sitting on the backs of distant camels.

Their rejection is an octave of presence, as it is for the perched falcon that is Vega, the predator staring from the northern quarter with its eyeball of lapis lazuli.

To navigate here is to surrender to these stars, to make use of their ineffable indifference. To journey, as if pillowed on their unconcern, through a region bereft of human fat.

Ashab

When he rubs the white stone in his pocket, the inscription—as illegible to the untrained eye as an Ogham epitaph on granite—invokes the gods at the source of Eridanus, who fire at the clouds with their blowpipes of mahogany. Suddenly, the rain is carried down the channel, which has been dry for years or possibly decades, causing the seeds to wake and blossom. The sand is covered in a mantle of greenness, stippled with polychromatic fragments. The seeds flower, set fruits and successor seeds, as if the act of magic guaranteed permanence.

The white stone in the pocket of the visitor acquires a film of protective dust. The flowers die—seeds are buried in sand, the flowering herbs are replaced by patterns the wind inscribes, the marks that are left by the hoof-prints of camels and the lasers of stars.

Brief periods of life are set amongst golden sleep, defining it to the visitor who walks away, remembering the superstitious Tuareg who had asked him to rub the white stone in his pocket for a sprinkling of rain. As he lives his life in the greenscapes of Europe, the clouds that are brought in from the Atlantic falter, melting, barely able to muster a drop of sizzling nourishment. They dissolve in the mirrors of the *chotts*, like Narcissuses stunned by the solid, salty sight that their reflections offer them.

Evidence: The Hoofprints of Camels

The sand is inscribed by the tracks of vehicles, but still no less by the hoofprints of camels. They convey the traders and the traded-in, and these prints express their patient, dry-mouthed masochism. They are beasts who expect nothing and are ready for all contingencies, yet can throw a tantrum over the smallest human infraction.

Yet the smallest mark also impresses the traveller. A piece of bone can bake for a hundred years. A trace of an old campfire can outlast its creators, and the couple who crept out secretly to lie, entwined, beside it, exuding moist heat in the fingernail-cracking dryness, are preserved by their faded shapes, as if embossed on a sheet of beaten light.

Hoofprints, fire-pits, wheel-tracks, words. The desert's rhythms are produced from these instances, with infinite patience and interminable slowness—spread across space, they are strewn on maps of human attention. And the star-points join those of the sand-dunes. The she-Camel culminates, not the Great Bear of the Britons or the Winter Stag of the Urals, and she snorts and clumsies at the zenith, tethered against the black-skinned galaxy, as the *balises* constellate the sand and the brilliant bones preserve the past like the egg-sacs of fish on an ocean floor.

So, the music of the desert is constructed. It is not the orderly polyphony of more fertile regions. It is an assemblage of traces, a swarming unison in which the fragments cluster and coincide, the amplification of a deeper silence.

Dead or alive, there is always room for one more camel, or another *azalai* of words—from breve to breve, from silence to silence, we deposit the trails that will leave us behind.

Ahal

Messages are traced on the palm of your hand, in a script your hand is able to read more easily than your mind. The melody itself is produced from a single string—the conversation loops and coils and sidles around it, never straying too far from its purpose but dancing with it, one-liners like high-kicks. The women are not chattels here—they make their own choices, pass on their language, raise their own children with the help of their brothers. Adorned in dyes of yellow, white and red, they clap their hands to the *tindé* and sing, as the goat whose skin is stretched across the *tindé* sings, as the wind sings as it rattles the carrion feathers of the doum palm, as the stars sing overhead to the *fennec* prowling in the dunes, as the blood cells hum to each other, as the aviary sings in the forest of each lung, as the light sings moving from world to world. The metal jewellery sings on the neck and on the arms, the forehead and the ears. A world defines itself by singing and letting the song hang loose, a branch that dips to silence.

As *litham*-clad men with shields of gazelle hide pay homage in the tent, your presence appears to pass unwitnessed—you are one of the *djenoun*, a dweller in empty places, an inhabitant of the night, here to gain a sense of what it means to be *out there*, in the centre of a vast, unbearably beautiful yet dangerous landscape, ten thousand Dartmoors stitched together and deprived of moisture. So you are stunned beyond language when a daughter of the *waran* leans across and scribbles a love-note on your upturned palm— "Come in from the cold" she says, mocking you gently with the pads of her sable fingers, enticing the writer into the writing, the soul back into the body, the hand to the breast where the desert is no more barren than the densest of forests. Kissing is unknown here, but that threshold has already been crossed—the magical spells of difference have been worked.

L'art rupestre

Those flayed hide pigments tether their prey to the rock wall. But the hunters have gone down into the sleep shelter, leaving behind no language, foxing us with these triangular images—cartoon depictions of a lost reality that we cannot even see behind us, in which the stars are skewed and the hippopotamus wallows in the swamps of the Ténéré.

Ten thousand years later, and the glyphs continue—the taurine epoch commemorated in a tawny swathe of ochres, as if there were no history to this, no more than signs expressed for the sake of expression alone, a herd of aurochs that blindly charges into the semiotic circus-ring. But when the eye bestows its magic, then the dead come back to life in that theatre of bright water, under the stars that set the world in the wide-open firmament.

To inspect these images is to find oneself standing one instant beyond the suspension of time, at a point where everything has already happened and the eye is a tachyon, travelling faster than the light which feeds it, always becoming more and more distant—as with the stars that feed the eye then change, sometimes fading, sometimes swelling, sometimes even exploding.

So, from outside, one is offered tomorrow in the desert. One stands bare-footed on the blade of the landscape, exposed, besieged, denied and tightened into a body-space that lets the outside reach its maximum size. One shrinks to a point, a grain of sand with a pin-prick of an eye, that remains as if the eye of a figure on that cave-wall at La Tefedest, white laser's aperture that can stare out past the present into the horizon's wall, can see to the far side of its own extinction. Its share of the gaze, this deathless death.

Mourzouk

The body's fear becomes golden. Something in the body, which is called 'the mind' but consists of a brain that falls to earth in a parachute of nerves, is splayed out in heat. The distance is reduced to the space between two pincers, but the body shines. Antares ascends at nightfall, casting its hematite net across the dunes. Towards morning, the arc-lamp of Mercury rises, paraffin-pink, between the constellations and the sun . . . but the body shines at dawn, is a golden gap that trembles.

Sun-side, shadow-side—the same exposure. Skin ground down to ashes and light. Walk here even in imagination, and one is exposed, impaled, on tomorrow's side of everything. Here, one is under the spotlight of the One—living from moment to moment by grace, in a constancy of confrontation, where the pulse of thirst repeats itself with the terror of the first time.

Thirst exists at every level of the need pyramid. And there are fears at all levels—that the water will only prolong the agony, that familiarity will smother all miracles, that the One has no love to share with the Many, that the effort is doomed and one can only await one's eventual desiccation. So the dunes of Mourzouk hold both promise and threat— they allow the gods of thirst to express their divinity, whilst offering them the obliteration not normally imposed on gods. They offer all, at the risk of withholding everything.

So fear emerges, a burning water flowing between two cliffs, swelling to the point where it is the river, not the banks, that are noticed. To row through the desert, on a river of this nature, torments the traveller. But one is cast into that honey-coloured space, exposed and called as if to account, where any hiding-place would immolate the intruder.

So, the moonwalk walked in dreams on the dunes of Mourzouk. One faces what is—one's impending death. One walks, leaves footprints which are steadily blown away. Yet one is briefly golden, here on the golden ground of the silent sand.

II

from *Strangers' Goods*

Getting the Taste Back

There's always something else, I convince myself. Some nuance of light, some horizon never before glimpsed, etc. Or a building hitherto un-noticed, an unwitting misprint, a pigeon's carcass wodged into a drain or a needle on the steps of a monument. Keep your eyes open, and you'll find it.

I remind myself of this, as I board the Devonport bus on the hunt for detail. From Whitleigh Green, the platinum smear of the Tamar shines. St Chad's, in its scuffed Fifties brick, is like a warehouse for a god that's shaped like a Spitfire. Past its counterpart, St Aidan's, the Co-op in Ernesettle is open, but the newsagent's protected by a metal screen. Uphill, a turn of the head reveals the confluence of Tamar and Tavy, the right-hand river rushing down from the moor. From King's Tamerton—and all this detail, I accept, means nothing to the uninvolved—the dockyard cranes are at rest on the river's edge. Camel's Head, Albert Road . . . the names creep past.

Getting off at Stonehouse Bridge, I loop back on myself, heading past boatyards and the white-walled marina, detouring as usual to the Scott monument and its desperate, splendid insignia. The pool at Mount Wise is drained, although there's a slick of discoloured water in its lower reaches. Turning away from the waxwork of King William, I note the unsurprising fact that the Little Mutton Monster is still closed, and that the cryptic message, Pig Are Gay, is still aerosoled on its boarded-up façade. The flats in James Street await demolition although the towers, reclaimed, display their pastels as they rise fifteen storeys into the winter afternoon. Turning at the Bristol Castle, I pass the monument and its crust of litter, head down Ker Street between the Egyptian House and a row of tenements. Eating the detail—it's a couple of years since I walked through this area—on the lookout for new signs, new points of departure, I begin to resume connection.

The wall of the South Yard will come down soon, and the two halves of Devonport will be joined once more. Millions have been invested although, as yet, the demolition is what one notices most. Down towards Cornwall Beach, a heap of rubble towers beside a luminous orange digger, the remains of the Cannon Street flats. Names take over here once more—Duke and Queen and Ordnance—in a landscape of B-movie muscle and trashed pomp. The shops that remain in Marlborough Street are as humble as the names are grandiloquent.

I get the taste back totally as I sit on a bench in Devonport Park, eating a *pain au chocolat* from the Spar Shop in Marlborough Street—surprised at my surprise at finding it good.

Town

The pigeon-chewed fabric is exposed now. Brutal appliances of demolition skulk as, outside Costa Coffee's newest outlet, tomorrow's mall rats stare towards the ripped-out innards of Burtons. I turn to face that mess, in my five-year old coat purchased there, in a hole in the sky with absent hangers, and think of the books I bought in Chapter and Verse, back in the late Seventies in Plymouth's only cultural bookshop—Celan, Ekelöf, Paz, all purchased in a space that will never again exist.

In two years' time, the Big Names will trade where seagulls quarter the sky. The raw materials will be shuffled again, to produce a sense of home, of excitement, of the conquered atmosphere—storeys will reach up, acquire plate glass and pouting assistants, and the rain and wind will ensure its success. Space to non-space to space . . . a schiz-flow of mirrors we cannot drown in.

The story of my life here is the story of spaces sucked into my mind, like the backdrops for Rilkean angels with Demnport accents. My parents are old enough to recall the pre-war street plan, the craters in the ground, the laying of foundation stones and the Khatchurianesque sweep of Royal Parade at its most pristine, like a trumpet blast from Soviet heaven—the marching bands, the flowers, the flags, the cauterised summer air. I recall the brighter stones of my own childhood, the post-war vision still fresh at a time of genuine full employment. Now, with the murals beginning to rot, the sutures widening, I am anchored to the city's re-aging, to the tissues of image-pulp inside my head.

Likewise, other spaces . . . Home Park before the re-development, those flimsy green seats bolted onto the terraces where I had stood two hundred times . . . or the clammy dark aquarium on the Hoe that gave way to the smooth curves of the family-friendly, interactive, so-many-pounds-a-ticket version. Memory tanks full of spectral sharks . . . in one I watch Pele with 38,000 others, Mike Dowling's goal from thirty-five yards and thirty-one years repeating itself in a fuzz. In another, I guide a girlfriend of brief duration past the sea bass and cuttlefish, so concerned at every word that I talk in a bouillabaisse of my own design. Inside, unreal, is a 'town' that nobody else can use.

Dizzy with fumes of evaporated time, I find a seat in its latest seal of approval. The air of the mall to come awaits its catharsis, drifting around my body as the mystery tramp conducts himself, like a self-wrapped mummy, in the direction of the Sundial. Opposite, the exposed walkways and cankerous panels continue to hang strangled in wiring.

Perhaps they could leave it like this . . . we could all get used to impermanence more easily than under normal conditions. As milky coffee solidifies in my cup, shoppers look up at the mall-dream to come and tomorrows I will never know occur to me, from the outside, as smiling and opaque as a clown's face of candy.

Crawl

The city dreams of itself, like any city, in a number of ways. The pirate—or 'privateer'—is one such way. Another is the jolly fisherman, who rounds us up for the Dockyard and the Warships on a bright afternoon—that one I don't dislike. I also rate the stiff-upper-lipped heroic version, the tented, frostbitten writer of journals—but that one belongs to all humanity. On the other side, however, there's the crew-cut thug, the stamper on heads, who has nothing he wants to contribute apart from his own thuggishness. And there's the woman in love with his muscles. More felicitous is the rounded, middle-aged female survivor who caws goodbye to her mates as she catches a bus back to the suburbs. The sailor or marine is of course a visitor, the city's dream of its Other rather than its Own. But the dream-shape I assume this evening is that of the merman, tail altered, piscine tendencies no less in evidence.

So I flop down Kinterbury Street, bus station on the one side, Job Centre on the other. At the Minerva, the usual Breughelesque crowd is eroding body space, so I settle for a half of cider downed in seconds via the back of the throat. At Porters, there's more room, so I ask for a double Southern Comfort and amaze a member of the bar staff by requesting ice, just that, no Coke or Tonic or Bovril. At the Queen's Arms, there is time to lounge in a newly-knitted cardigan and listen to a man berate his girlfriend for nothing in particular, or because her shadow is flirting, unbeknown to both of us, with my own slim shadow. As I crawl to the Dolphin, the salt begins to gather in the tide-pools under the street-lamps. The plaster floor's as slippery as the deck of a wreck left stranded on the Eddystone reef. Even the punters smell of iodine, and the Plymouth Gin that I quaff is as oily as a mackerel.

Beyond the Mayflower Steps, and Dutton's Restaurant, and the tinkling masts and wobbling lights, I find myself a quieter watering hole where hake and gurnard nuzzle the tankards of the dead. I would never go there in the flesh, but there is a part of me that can scuttle, easily, along the seabed in the company of crabs. It's all too simple . . . the sky becomes as green as a forest.

I keep walking, drinking, gathering salt in my bloodstream. Skirting the Breakwater, passing Rame Head, I come ashore at the Eddystone in a lonesome strobe. Holding up my hand, I project shadow-signals, creatures of shade, towards the land that scintillates with its liquid lights.

I round off the evening at Kitty O'Hanlon's, amongst students in replica strips, and on a bed of sawdust bearing a faint odour of the ocean that I can taste, myself, on the mare's tails and breakers of a pint of Guinness. Later, there's a laurel wreath of seaweed, caught in my hair, that no-one appears to notice and which lands on the empty seat of the bus beside me—at which point I return to myself, the city's salt-encrusted Tarot intact.

Observation

If I stand on the Hoe, and look towards the Eddystone lighthouse—visible, in good weather, at around fifteen kilometres—I take in a sea that changes its colour like any sea, on which a selection of sailing craft, from warships and the Roscoff ferry down to the smallest dinghy, can be seen at almost any time of the year. If it's a clear night, I will look out across a random array of lights, which will not reflect, but complement the constellations. The line of the Breakwater, with its sea-cage and obelisk, is only clearly visible by day, and the beam of the lighthouse will be too far off to observe with ease. Nonetheless, it will be doing its job.

Beyond the Eddystone—if approached at a certain angle from the Hoe—a sight-line might extend over several thousand miles of water, through the gap between the Canary Islands and the shores of Morocco, through the much greater gap between the islands of the South Atlantic and the southern African coast, to touch land—or ice—again in the Antarctic. It follows, therefore, that if I shift my attention just a fraction to the right or left of the narrow needle of the lighthouse, I may see straight through to Antarctica, to the place where this city's unluckiest hero perished, where his bones are interred even now.

If I look in that direction, knowing this, getting the sight-line exactly right . . . then the icebergs will rise on the southern horizon, and the other side of the world, the cairn he is under, will be as near to me as the thirty-times-as-far-away moon. I might even wake up tomorrow, in a possible world in which Plymouth, overnight, has drifted across the line to begin, again, on the coast of Graham Land where bergs parade and penguins assemble. I might even see Scott, as I shiver myself to death, with Bowers and Wilson as they lumber up Armada Way man-hauling their memoirs, as a walrus-gummed glacier gleams in the direction of Kit Hill.

Back at Bretonside Bus Station—as if by way of contrast—the choreographies of the mystery tramp continue. He paces, not in a circle but in a series of staccato marches, as if inscribing a sigil on the ash from four decades of cigarette butts. In this all-but-derelict space long overdue for replacement, he paces in his long soiled overcoat, his coarse hair hanging from the threadbare moon of his scalp. Despite the occasional sighting elsewhere in the City Centre, this appears to be the core of his world, this contracted space where pigeon discharge drops to the flagstones. I conclude that he is the extra man of Shackleton's party—horrified by the white-outs, keen above all else to hide, to pace off his obsessions in this unfortunate sanctum.

Perhaps his fellow-explorer will emerge, to the moraine-like sound of an organ lodged in an orchestra, with nothing more or less tragic than a trail of pony bones behind him. As if we could all sail back, in the end. I imagine him scraping his skis by the photo booth, moving, in recognition, to the domain of ritual.

III

Inland

Source

Stoke Climsland, July 2001

To rise, with the landscape swimming in itself, the line of hills appearing to melt to the west. To escape the littoral, at last, for the summit that leads to the source land over the hill.

*

In the foreground, the fence posts peel. In the background, the anorexic stack of the Kit Hill monument rises. In the invisible distance beyond them both, the Long Men of prehistory are encamped, as these are, in the tussocky grass.

*

Thin twigs twist over auburn bracken, set against the sherbet explosions of the moor-grass. Skylarks nest, nailed down by the heat.

*

Sunlight riddles the back of the head. The landscape sheds its moisture— even its song subsides. The hill looks out on something in the process of turning grey, then white, then transparent. The pulse falls, as if over the edge of a ravine.

*

Stalks vector over ferns, following the grain of an endless pattern. The earth reaches into the sky, but flattens in the face of that paradox. The ferns are the ghosts of fallen birds, that mimic their lives of flight as in the Hades seen by the lyrist.

*

The column stands on a shaggy hillock at the summit. People sit on its lower steps and bask in the view, as a black dog chases a scent that is just as intense and far-reaching. A motion of the hands might cause it to topple, altering the lie of the landscape—disturbing the detective who is sniffing out the props of this particular theatre.

*

The column lets the invisible stars revolve around it, as the blanched blue sky divests itself of its final cloud-scraps. Even the gorse has the clarity of crystal—its flowers are trapped in a moment that outlasts them. They bend beneath the weight of white admirals, where weakness is the ghost of acceptance.

*

Scrawled on the wall of a quarryman's hut—*Kernow Agan Bro*. But what appears to be the Gwenn Ha Du—the white and black of the Cornish flag—is in fact a narrow grille in the wall of the building, where the king, the saviour, lies sleeping with his bracken-haired knights.

*

Over the hills, the roofs of Launceston are glinting. The Devonport tower blocks loom from the estuarine haze in their obliterated pastels. Near and far—two wings of a magpie, stealing all unity.

*

Here, the ground below is given a role at the surface. Everything is flushed out of its hiding place, whether by the sheets of rain that cover the ground in autumn, or the sun that ripens, then blanches the dock-leaves. Even the sky is exposed, to the ground behind the sky, the place where language widens into presence.

*

A special *airiness* graces the northern slopes—suffusing the quarries, the great green sails of the fields that stretch from one moor to another. The landscape is fastened to the earth by human constructions—the granite towers of the parish churches, the mine-stacks that flock in the midst of pastures. The oaks that intersperse the hedges, by contrast, are an ephemeral embroidery.

*

A glance back at the monument reveals its construction, its stage-set phallocentrism—as if it were possible to fertilise the sky, through this patient penetration.

*

Mine-stacks, quarries . . . the landmarks of lost effort. The *inevitability* of these silent chimneys, green-bearded as the fragments of a ship whose form may no longer be guessed, but which sails on the underside, as laden as ever.

*

To be crystalline, in a landscape rich with foreboding.

*

The immense green patchwork stippled with oaks extends into the interior. One peels back ridge after ridge in search of the centre, the country where all is remote, yet intimate and always spacious. After doing so a dozen times, one reaches the other shore . . . and that is all there is.

*

The lane down whitens in heat and light. The enormous country spreads, as if lit from below as well as above.

*

This is the land behind the hill, where the curve of the fields is illumined by the stranger's gaze. It is named in secret. To be there, is to defer to stranger gods, to let the sun colonise the broken image of another earth.

*

There are tracks that leave the forehead exposed . . . chimneys rising into the white expanse. What *can* it mean to say, "This is my country?"

*

Descending through hedged lanes to the hamlet of Downgate, the parish church visible where the hedges part, one is conscious of going deeper into an imagined past, as if about to confront a steadily-stranger line of ancestors. The costumes become more archaic as the lane grows woolier, as the hedges rise still further, as the silence hardens in heat.

*

One crossroads, amongst so many, is gently lowered into hedges that are higher than any man has ever stood. Luminous grey roofs perspire in the afternoon glare.

*

In a landscape of dock leaves, bindweed and celandine, the startling reds of public telephone boxes, now hardly used and ripe for removal, are as abrupt as the sapphire butterflies that drift past, causing the eyes to spring from their leashes. Both suck up the light in unfamiliar ways, like adjectives swimming in a pool of nouns.

*

Red Devon cattle graze in a Cornish field . . . one or two staring, the others feasting on starch and chlorophyll. They are tethered by shadow, extensions of larded mud—as sluggish as the stones that wall in their paddocks.

*

The parish church is taller now, an insect exposed on the tip of a fern—feeding on light, on the syrups of its own longevity.

*

A sparrow rises, succeeded by a butterfly so fast in its flight that what is left is the aftermath of blue, the ocean of the eye condensed to a sign. In the hedge, it pursues the imperatives of closure, too brief to be profligate.

*

At Old Mill, a cat glides out of a late Victorian cottage clad in a worn pink stucco. To find oneself in an armchair in that cottage, surrounded by low-key comforts—logs for burning, horseshoes nailed to the wall, a pot of tea stewed black—contained, withdrawn, at ease with the space between the cities and the void.

*

To assert presence, in the definite tense of other languages . . . *that* milk-churn, *that* mine-stack, *that* water, *that* silence. To struggle into that blank space, feeling the stratus weight of one's own demise.

*

"No Unauthorised Entry" reads the sign at the entrance to the farm at Mearfield. The gatepost is several feet high, and the gate opens into a short drive that leads to a two-storied granite barn. Cattle graze in a stall with a corrugated roof, and hay bales whiten in the yard. It is mad to make any kind of claim, to imagine my twelve- or fourteen-greats grandfather waking up, in a wooden cot, four centuries ago in the building before me.

*

Yet it is easier to imagine his "past" than it would have been for him to envisage my "future". We would appear to those who lived four hundred years ago as demons, weirdly attired, gigantic in size, at ease with our dark inventions, yet strangely inexpert in the skills that are needed for a human being to survive in their world. All notions of kinship would reside with us, alone.

*

This place, for me, is at an earlier stage than home. It is the place that denotes a deeper origin, one in which all current identity is implicit yet indecipherable. Origin is all but impossible to grasp—beyond this brief focus of stability, it continues to spiral, back to the Ice Age rovers, and the loping apes who searched for scraps in the Danakil Desert. Only sometimes, by an effort of will, it fixes its glittering eye upon the present's guests.

*

To see the herds home under the stars. To come to rest on the slope, watching the lights move over the hill.

*

In the foreground, a chicken cackles. The grey stones sleep. At the moment, the sun is constructing a church from fragments of landscape. It is made of granite, with a westerly tower that rises over the road. Nothing stirs—no dogs, no people. Stoke Climsland is embedded in the brilliant shade of secrecy.

*

Outside the post office, a car windscreen catches a shaft of light that tilts like a windmill. It is closed. There is no other shop, no pub. As I walk, I kick imaginary mothballs into the roadside. My footsteps seem heavier than usual—the flies are as obtrusive and as raucous as rooks.

*

The school is without its bell—its granite tower remains, like the dwarf imitation of a Breton bell-tower, made to last and act as a second focus for the village. The released bell chimes silently, as the absent children play in the lanes and race between stones.

*

Beside its glacial sculpture of a church, the graveyard is a thicket of names and rhythmic platitudes. The form of Kit Hill curves to the south, hiding the estuary, and the city beyond it, in a mirror image of the earlier reversal.

*

The inscriptions relate their ultimate settlements, the bargains sealed with the soil of this place beneath the flattened hump of the batholith. But a quick search, a glance at the war memorial and a ten-minute conversation with the verger reveals no namesakes, after all. The dissolution is complete . . . not tied to any memorial, the imagined memory wanders everywhere.

*

Yet to be laid to rest here, rotting into the clays of evening, is *not* to be located. To be located is to live, to resist location by the fact of one's movement, yet to find oneself located moment by moment. It is the dead who are laid in placelessness, yet suggest the source land that the living enter and leave, reject or seek.

Whim Round

Adding one's footprint, one's shadow, to the already intact. Subtracting one's breath, one's passage, one's penumbra—letting them rise into the upper air, like a squadron of kites.

*

There's a hole in my shoe—my eyes are smeared with the wind's Tabasco. The sky's milk is gaunt beneath my feet. 'The land exists, once upon a time and only, in the tomorrow of its ruins'—is just one of the sentences I bring here to test.

*

'Mirror of buzzards'—not eagles, as on Char's Mont Ventoux—this landscape of aftermath, in which I am blown upward to recline on my own means of escape.

*

Mineral traces in the vegetation on the surface—how photograph that? The wind has blown through, is blowing through, to leave the geomantic forms of its absence, in a *tabula rasa* that never was.

*

Whim Round—the circle a horse walked, in order to work winding gear, at Houseman's Shaft, Parson's or Prosper. Halfway up, I imagine the body of a clown on the springy turf, his nose pulled out of his face—and the sheep's corpse it resumes, suddenly, as the hawthorns semaphore to each other at my request.

*

"This is solid country," writes Peter Stanier, the author of *Minions Moor*. Meaning—some distance under the feet. Meaning glassy-grey to white quartz, white feldspar, black biotite, white muscovite, black tourmaline—bertrandite and phenacite, names I wouldn't recognise in stone if they crushed me. 'As above, so below' is only applicable to the extent that the copper seams and the heaven's filaments are one and the same, as they are.

*

Grace Dieu, Greenhill, Shelstone and Phoenix—the names torn out of the ground by the Old Men. A gold cup, over three thousand years old, was salvaged from Rillaton Barrow—but, until I can walk two metres beneath the surface, butting through solid earth and rock like an icebreaker prising whiteness apart, or a quarryman plugging and feathering the silver-toned granite, I will scratch these surfaces only.

*

The deads are at my feet as I labour north. The view from the Devil's Armchair, from the Lizard to Exmoor on a clear day, can cause the viewer to go mad, or be a poet, or both, after one night's exposure. It is not a clear day—I bite Fate's silver bullet and move on.

*

The boggy ground makes a marshland of shoes. One could sink here as on a bunch of tin, a leaving amongst time's leavings—and how carelessly the grass would spring back. From sett to sett, the tutworkers retreat, until the moor becomes a page no longer dressed by the bal maidens' hammers. So this was their 'tomorrow'—indeed. An uneven ground, where buzzards bring down their prey.

*

I follow the line of a stope, by way of the gangue strewn on the surface, from shaft to test pit—returning by gravity, like the long ripped-up Cheesewring railway, to the House of Blazes whose absent inn sign creaks in the wind that surpasses it. Circling, or looping rather, like a pantomime horse marooned on a stage, or led round and round by a sugar lump clenched in the hand of a fake princess. As if I could 'bring something back'.

*

Impending rain. And the horse breaks loose in its spotted costume, lolloping towards Stowe's Pound in a tattered advance. Becoming my body, to outflank my silence.

*

So I chase the wildcat away and over the moor. Or, rather, it gives me pleasure to write that sentence, which is logically possible.

*

Crab winches, designed to 'draw the stones into their proper places' still hang in the quarry, under the impish form of the Cheesewring. The results of this work can be seen in London, Portsmouth, even Calcutta—like familiar words, arranged in incomprehensible sentences.

*

I can't suck up the land with these words—so what am I taking away, and are you even here? The world, glossed over with greasepaint, attends the lasso-shaped ellipse.

*

But after the gold rush comes the land—the damp grass, the deads, the surface workings, the bent fescue—and, at its eastern edge, a magnificent engine-house looks over the valley, beyond Kit Hill to a skyline of tors. At its western edge, the ground falls away, from Craddock Moor to the waters of Siblyback.

*

I am minded to mould it in resin, like a Boyle family project on a grand scale, or the life-sized equivalent of the distorted relief map of Devon and Cornwall that hung in my form room thirty years ago. I shudder at writing that, at being an aftermath myself.

*

But, as ever, the ocean begins to close in, in the form of staggering rain. The beacon-tops along the long spine of the peninsula are fading, one by one, as yet another front turns everything grey and green. The spectres, ghosts and circus animals are gone. One circuit's sufficient—there are other Via Sacra to walk.

*

In Minions, I drink a large mug of tea and wait for a dry way down. The wildcat fells the pantomime horse, with a single bite to its neck—not here, not there, but in the absence that expresses itself in the word *between*.

Oubliette

spent time in the burgi di Lideforde

Taken in at a glance, the seigniorial dimensions—church, castle, and pub, granite cottages, a closed down post office (moved to the garage on the main road), a primary school and a War Memorial—reveal the village of Lydford. This is the former home of the mint-masters Aelfwine, Bruna, Saewine and Godwic, Devon's second city this time last millennium . . . the burh where they hammered out silver pennies, to be borne back to Swedish museums on long ships. Devon's Petra—a single worked-out seam of a street, with a name like a rabbit's skeleton pulled out of a hat.

*

As I tune in, sluggishly—chiselling at the afternoon's coign—a calligram suggests itself—

LYDA LYDAN LYDANF LYDE LYDEFORDE

LYDAFOR LYDFO LYDAFORD LYD LYDANFORDE

LYOA LYDANFORD LYNEFOR LHYD HILDAFORDA

LYDANFOI LYDEFO LYDAFON LHYDA ILLYDAF

Names march down the map, a waterfall of approximations. There are as many former names for this place (it seems) as inhabitants today.

*

In St. Petroc's Church—once so poor that snow fell on the holy table—I interrogate the brass eagle who has caaed, however silently, for much longer than I've breathed. St. Petroc summons his wolf in an old cartoon—a name, a sign, to play with. From here, the Lych Way and King Way reach towards higher ground, domains where the drifts no longer take place.

*

The spalliards and the meresmen, parcelling out the moor's turbary, come to ground in the notebook as if pickled in brine. The abundant birdsong's more real than the silenced cars in the street—madly, for a moment, I wonder if I could take a photograph that would encompass its music.

Instead, I enter the *immersive space* of the keep, the long-since-trashed control tower of twizzle-haired miners picking rabbit-shit from their gums. At least you're safe in here from the Gubbinses, with their horrible carmine beards, from the men of the vyndefelde who'll turn anything to charcoal—or from the portreeves with their silver seals as heavy as neutron stars. A terrain that power consumes provokes my retreat, to the black space at its core where ringdoves patrol.

*

The water drips through moss that could be a pollen-trap for ghosts—the walls are also covered with sour green lichen and slivers of cobweb. In one of the dungeons—an oubliette, to which there is no way down apart from a push or a jump—two Budweiser bottles lose their molecules with unimaginable slowness.

*

Pinning my eyes to the gravel, I invoke the prisoners . . . their thousands of days of chained discomfort, punctuated only by the drips from the damaged lead roof that betokened death and the threat of eternal agony to follow in a hell already prepared. But all I can do is leave a space for their re-entry, holding my tongue as if in suppression of judgement—looking up at the stripped-off roof, at the shield of sky that was dented by their souls.

*

And the past shrinks, like the importance of this place, to become a star-field of dwarves. In the ju-ju-pink-painted Castle Inn, later, the real thing appears—to the left of the bar, two silver pennies from the reign of Ethelred the Unready, in a glass display case mounted on the wall, bring the vapours back to earth.

*

I am here to recall what I do not own. The coinage still settles in the tills of the inn, but the estrays are no longer sequestered in the pinhold behind it. The lodes are strewn, the soltidown faythers buried for good. What is possessed here hangs back, embedded or stockpiled. On clear winter nights, the moon will spill its sediments in the shade of the *noyse of the water*, leaving mirrors of ice in old depressions.

IV

Six Strokes for Fernand Khnopff

I Lock the Door upon Myself

Silent, in an ancient house, he gazes at rafters as the evening tilts its wing. Despite the laudanum in both air and blood, at one second past the end of the world, his addiction's not to opiates but silence. Twilight fails as the window's ink runs over its surface—the smudged canal and worn-down cobbles vanish from view. Crows perch, chewing on the pale sun's ashes. Fog rises from smoky water, greying the air. This house is filled with books that articulate dust, but he's too much in love with the silence to read, for fear of *reading aloud*. In the absence of a companion, he is both male and female, living and dead, and everything succumbs to his backward glance . . . the crow-stepped house outlasting its ships, the moon in ascent through a waste of weeds. He gazes into chiaroscuro, the world summed up in a book too onerous to be written. Any motion, even of the hand, would be a sacrilege.

The Accoutrements of Silence

Gone are the splintered ships with fusty cargoes—gone to the bottom, gone to other ports, to chronicles that no-one deciphers. This city's greys and browns remain stronger than any single life, despite this loss, yet no less finite. There may even come a time when it exists as a rumour, spectral bells apportioning silence in spaces between the wounds of the plough. This evening, it is out at sea again but by way of the fog brought in from the sea, across the flatlands, past the windmills, mussel-stalls and amusement arcades—cocooned in miasma, it is by-passed by motorways and flight paths alike. How decrepit its experience—faded words in a scrolled and over-embellished language—its wielders of power reduced to devoted couples chiselled on tombs. If time could end, then death would complete the picture and the picture would be no more splendidly pointless than this. Jewels in thick mud, crowns in troughs, the winnowing of dust from dust and the scrape of a scythe with the smile of a god.

Self-Portrait, with Masks and Ashes

The secret and its reflection, concealed in lanes of a melancholy town left high and dry by the water's retreat, are accessible, exclusively, to those who walk in circles, on empty Sunday afternoons in November, when only bars are open and loners stagger home with circles of peat around their eyes. In walking to discover one acquires the mask that the secret wears, becomes the remnant of a masked procession wearing the heads of eels and the tails of ravens . . . stumbling over the sound of bells that reverberates from cobbles with the harshness of lead. Playing the part of a shabby, overlooked detective, exiled to this provincial recess for an unspecified transgression, one searches canals for suicides but finds instead cigarette lighters, porno mags and the corpses of rats. So walks, increasingly frenzied . . . seeing oneself distorted, thinking of moments stacked behind the head like a pyramid of padlocks ready to fall, to crush the spirit for good.

Adoration of the Mystic Lamb

The city, idealised in oils, seems much younger than the one outside the museum. But step out and the two are con-mingled. Wimples, hose, chain-mail, rags, smells so enormous as to smother clouds. Scars on the backs of penitents, lepers hidden in corners waiting to be expelled, hint at a life more vivid, brief and raw than modern perception can accommodate, a life lived in the presence of angels and demons. Today, it's execution time again, and vendors at the foot of the scaffold sell exquisite pralines. Fashion statements from Antwerp mingle with sackcloth, as if anorexic models had returned to the past as succubae, their handbags laden with the treasures of Dis. On the scaffold, an outcast prays in his guttural native language to a heathen deity. The Just God appears in a lamb's-wool cloud and lowers his hand in pursuance of order. But the nightmare of history becomes the subject of dream-control, to the sound of bells, harmoniums, an oboe like a wading bird in the trance of its strut . . . when the witch on the adjoining scaffold utters a thrombosis of vowels, the woodworm attack.

Sleeping Medusa

Reach out to touch her, through veils the colour of air, and the softness becomes a painful memory—the hair is spun copper and the lips corundum. She knows, withdrawing the tenderness of her gaze to replace with basilisk. She knows, and is inscrutable, she holds her pose despite the collapse, in a city made of shadows, water and exhausted gold. Her wings, believed in, seem imposed, their texture between the feathers of an owl and the metal of a breastplate. They are an extension of her frown—they move to erase an apologetic world and replace it with a blasted, black-grounded void. She will bestow you on this city as a statue, worn beyond bone in the recess of a church in a back lane fringed with webs. She is relentless—once you are dust, she will grind the dust in her talons to insult the passage of time. The bells of the city ring above your head, the crows convene and the moon surmounts the western sky like a mattock of sulphur. The last thing you will remember is the bottomless pit of your stomach.

Central Belgium in the Dark

after the music of Univers Zero

Trains traverse the acreage of night . . . between gaps in their curtains farms in wide, flat fields are visible, attended by poplars. Small towns appear and vanish—with belfries and spacious squares, unique varieties of beer—and Europe not only begins but deepens. But the dead walk, no, stagger through this landscape like drunkards, begging forgiveness for sins that no-one gave a damn about in the first place . . . they weep into foggy canals, assemble in empty places and count themselves endlessly, night after night, in dozy roll-calls as insomniac travellers head for Aachen and beyond. They are all regretful—*none of them caressed the flanks of the Sphinx.* This is why they cannot leave for the underworld. Life should have been enough but it was not, and scrapings of old music pull at their spectral ears. So this plain accommodates the whining of the dead, their clueless attempts at turning back the clock . . . and, night after night, as pigs fart in a thousand sheds, as oysters snore in crates, they flagellate themselves and drag absurd, invisible shadows over the flatland.

V

from *Inscriptions*

Osmosis

Chasing the city through the city, I plot a course through its quarters, inscribing another pattern that can be traced on its street-map—not a deliberate Hawksmoor sigil, but a shape that's almost autistic in its detachment from geometry. It's the shape of a day spent soaking up the evidence, from the touched-up facades of Dankó utca to the closed Cafe Lukács, from the falafel outlet at the Al Amir to the benches, outside the metro at Deák tér, where pigeons comb a mound of bare earth, in search of bugs, like Roundheads conducting a house-to-house search in a costume drama.

I'm simultaneously engaged and bored. There's no pretence at sightseeing on my part on a day like this, no further motivation to pick out plums from the metropolitan pie. If I'm straining for new insights, things that haven't been revealed by earlier visits or by similar streets, they'll be found by serendipity and won't ever make the guidebooks.

Inside my head, another street-map becomes more detailed. I can refer to it whenever I want—for example, if I happened to be typing this out at home, on a Sunday morning, two thousand kilometres to the west. At times, it resembles an immaculately-scaled model, seen through slightly frosted glass, at other times something assembled, blindly and randomly, with string, wire, Plasticine and glues of equine heritage. In either case, it exists and answers to 'Budapest'—the name of the city. Nor, of course, do I take from the city in order to acquire it.

So what can be done with this information—and what value is it to others? The *flâneur* considers this, if at all, in hindsight. The first thing she or he thinks of is the pleasure of traversing ground, on the trail of a quarry that can never be caught. The city flows into the mind but, conversely, the mind flows into the city and transfigures its accretions—as if, in the last resort, a single substance was possible, and had emerged. Within that context, one step succeeds another, one sight supplants another and a line is inscribed, an indelible signature of anonymity.

Dancing the Palimpsest

As I walk, the city returns its sounds and images—imprinting itself more firmly on the four-dimensional map beneath my forehead.

In Erzsébetváros—the site of the former ghetto—the streets are canyons of beige and ochre. A hundred years of graft and angst have turned them into secular cloisters, places where it's hard not to meditate . . . on corner shops, graffiti'd doorways, wizened plants in turquoise tubs, litter bins and entry phones. Afternoon wears to a stub. Someone's drawn a heart on a building in chalk, where a Star of David might have been, to peel in its own good time. Signs rust on buildings—'Rolux Fény', 'Olcsó Ruk' . . . traces accumulate like shells of a humble, enigmatic creature.

How many possible routes does this city provide, amounting to the same, anonymous ecstasy? In a place so many-faceted, a hour's walk will exhaust the feet more emphatically than the mind. I enunciate balconies, stucco laurels, rusted shutters and ripped-up fragments of poster, surrounded by people I pretend to recognise.

A shopping bag, in the national colours of red, white and green, acts as a talisman in busier locales . . . warding off 'consume girls', Hari Krishna charity collectors and other tourists seeking directions. Here, its status is neutral—I bear it like a flag of convenience on which, unusually, the image of a flag is printed. A Union Jack would be no more or less conspicuous . . . I am not a foreigner here, but an intruder. There's a subtle difference and I've crossed that line.

Moving from street to street, by way of semi-random decisions that are nonetheless aimed at the busy boulevard of Andrássy út, I insinuate myself into the urban fabric—again, my trajectory crosses that of at least two million others, including you. As on the poster advertising a language school I saw, that time, unexpectedly at the top of the metro staircase, you seem to appear in the corner of my eye, or ahead of me on the opposite side of the road . . . manifesting where I look, but only to vanish. So, the city comes to hold, not only my solo narrative, but the words of our story.

Dead Men's Shoes

On the Pest bank of the Danube, near Parliament House, there are iron shoes in pairs . . . their owners, who never wore them in their lives, were shot from the bank in the autumn and winter of 1944-45 for the capital crime of being Jewish. The patriots of the Arrow Cross committed this deed, under the Árpád flag now rehabilitated at political demonstrations—then, and now in some hands, it was a symbol of a Turanian wonderland unsullied by Semites, Roma, and interlopers from the mongrel Atlantic. They did so as, on the Buda bank, the *turul*-bird of Magyar legend perched proudly on the Castle Hill walls . . . and either exalted in their ruthlessness or, with a certain degree of resignation, performed a solemn yet, in their minds, unavoidable act of national hygiene.

Sixty years later, they are despised by all apart from the most intransigent of fascists, and Budapest—both a Hungarian city and a Jewish one—is, above all else, a city that belongs to the world. But these iron shoes, scattered on the bank in a quiet place without traffic, where cheap leather shoes were taken off before the shots rang out from behind, speak of utter homelessness. They are worn by ghost-people with invisible yellow stars who act, as witnesses, to suffering and ignominious death. They express the vulnerability of human beings in the face of armed barbarity, but also the possibility—the possibility only—of eventual vindication and memorial.

They are not shoes of a kind I am ever likely to wear, although this has often been said. They are not shoes of a kind my friends are ever likely to wear, although this has been said, as often, and with less conviction.

Chastened by seeing them, unexpectedly, on an iron-blue day beside the Danube I continue north—tempted, despite my exhaustion, to cross the next bridge. It's as if I were expecting to see wet footprints on the opposite bank.

White Steps

Limestone chips, the size of dice, roll beneath the feet on the way down. Away from the road, the crowds around stalls that sell strudel, the avaricious hotel restaurant and the bus bay, it's possible to walk, encountering only the occasional mushroom-picker or jogger, crossing a railway line whose tickets are punched by children. In a clearing called Virág-völgy—The Valley of Flowers—a wooden picnic table is surrounded by low, hard seats and entices wasps, even this late in the year. Beech, oak, sky, heartbeat. A sudden silence, incomplete, is imagined so. The clamorous noise of the city to the east subsides.

Suddenly, Central Europe is a single forest stippled with stockades and traders in bearskin hats. Wolves chase birds, events un-happen and the sound of an aircraft passing overhead becomes the sonic surge of an eagle or a falcon. Potions are stirred and correspondences re-discovered. Life becomes vast, precarious and mythical, in the march of a Gilgamesh or the descent of a Persephone.

Walking for an hour, no more than a few hundred metres from the road and the TV transmitter, one senses what it meant to be a single shadow surrounded by the overlapping shadows of tree-trunks. No longer can the rush of the sea be heard. Land is infinite, in wave upon wave of turquoise hills. One walks, rests, dies and wolves tear out the lights and the tongue.

Walking into the past and the future . . . walking out of the system, *as if.* A suddenly-tattered and defenceless man, on a calcite path, at risk from every side and intoning prayers to St Christopher, yet splendidly poised and deeply at ease. The world begins with his skin, at last. Make way for the peregrinating fool!

And this temporary sense, this conceit of errant knighthood, is taken down into the city. This path continues under the feet, leading to a death more resonant, more generous, than he had ever imagined.

Paradise

In a *hortus conclusos* at Visegrád, there are Lion and Hercules Fountains—window reliefs of 'angels and wild men', where the future Count was imprisoned by the wise, alchemical king who caused the shepherdess Ilona (Helen) to perish from love. But there's insufficient time to linger—whereas Dracul did so for a decade, there are only four hours in this case. So it's uphill, over bumpy limestone paths so steep as to narrow the lungs, to a renovated castle two hundred metres above the sky-blue Danube . . . where blue-green hills recede towards the Carpathians, and red-white summer houses catch the sun on the northern hillside. And, after ice tea (peach and blackcurrant), there's a further climb, with a gentler gradient, to a look-out tower that's closed, no doubt for 'technical reasons'—not far from its rusted lock, a lizard flashes, zig-zag-rune-like, from stone to stone.

The woods on my map surround the blue-marked trail to Pilisszentlászló, that I would take if I had a day to spare . . . and knowing that I have to descend, so soon, revives my melancholia. Descending the Calvary path, I leave this *paradiso terrestrium* behind, with its narrative of 'decades' and 'centuries' I can only abuse in a single afternoon. Then a raven polices the verge, where I wait for a bus in the company of a local labourer, some Chinese tourists, a teenage girl and a father and child. I look back at the palace, the tower of Solomon, the castle high on the hill and it is no time at all since I arrived.

Vlad Dracul, on his last day here . . . what would he have felt, relief or regret? Earlier, he would have strolled, a caged chimera, from fountain to fountain and chafed at hospitality. The sagacity of Mátyás would have irked and impressed him . . . here was a king with a mighty library, who had never even left a silver goblet in an empty square as proof of omnipotence. I think of the conversations they might have had, the hard cop and the soft, debating the wiles of statecraft in this best of all possible places . . . time betrayed them, too, and the dust from their graves is finely suspended in the air that each one of us inhales.

Paradise is the place one leaves, knowing that one leaves, knowing that one leaves surprisingly, shockingly older . . . whether by ten years, or an afternoon.

Superimpositions

The second-class only, stopping train proceeds to Szolnok, past Gyömrö, Tápiószecsö, Nagykáta and Újszász. Outside, an undulating, arable landscape gives way to the western fringe of the *puszta*—inside, in a comfortable carriage, I listen to a gentle clatter of moments in motion, growing older with minimum abruptness.

As I sit and meditate on the landscape, the place-names, the faces on platforms, a four-part, twenty-minute track, from 1970 or thereabouts, comes into my head. I recognise it as 'Split', by the Groundhogs—a piece I probably haven't heard for at least a decade. Snatches of each section appear simultaneously, overlapping and tangling, with the exception of the second of the four—I have to take time to recall this, trying out connections, fragments, possible riffs and timbres. In the end, however, the piece emerges entire, and accompanies me throughout the rest of the journey.

There's something about the rumble of their music, for this listener at least, that evokes the wide open skies and long horizons of the East of England. Much of rural Hungary, particularly east of the Danube, is redolent of what, for me, is the far side of Britain, a terrain I now know even less well than that of the *puszta* . . . so the connection is clear, if only in my mind, and the Groundhogs succeed, this April morning, in blowing Bartók off-stage.

Later, in Szolnok's town museum—empty, apart from several attendants and myself—there's a magnificent painting by László Mednyánsky, of storm-clouds over a crow-dark field. The prophet of 'Sátántangó', the convincing Irimiás, walks through that field a hundred years later.

I think of how the Groundhogs drew their inspiration from the blues of the Mississippi Delta. Wide skies, portents, freight trains and crossroads. I imagine Tony McPhee, the lead guitarist, in the guise of the post-impressionist Mednyánsky—whose likeness I have never seen— holding a paintbrush (not a plectrum) as he waits, for dusk, in the flat and fertile lands of the Delta 'where the Southern cross the Dog'. If hellhounds break from their chains, then who can prevent them heading all the way to Spilsby or Szolnok? Safe in the nearer west, I revise these lines.

Fata Morgana

The *puszta* resists the glance bestowed, indulgently, on eventful landscapes. A two-hour journey offers flat green field-strips, distant windbreaks, an occasional farmhouse, dusty towns with rusty Soviet-era railway stations and silos.

It calls to mind an enormous map, on the scale of one-to-one, spread by a giant on the floor of a building so vast as to contain its own allowance of clouds. As if there were nothing but map, on which the train, so narrow and tall, is like a mountain in motion.

Not every landscape changes at the speed of thought, or sates the obsessive desire to gaze on novelties . . . sometimes, after all, the sky will take up much more space than the flat, unchanging earth. But what would it be like to live on a map the size of a landscape, seeing only the four directions under skies that rise to an invisible ceiling?

Debrecen is a welcome relief, a caesura on a journey whose only fitting destination would be a yurt on the Kazakh steppe. But, despite the pastel cheeriness of Piac utca (Market Street), the austerity of the Nagytemplom reflects that of the *puszta*—paying homage to a stern white god whose silence is ominous. The simplicity of the layout suggests an image of deep space in negative. Blue trams patrol, leviathans of the randomly-damned in a city of Calvinist acumen. This is an island republic in a sea of dying sunflowers, drowning in air that turns them to dross.

The return journey passes even more slowly, as I drift into a beery trance. Then—near Szolnok—a dog stands still, on a concrete ramp surrounded by girders, blocks of stone and overhead wires. I can't imagine him chewing a bone or chasing a rat. If he exists, he does so as a *fata morgana*, hallucinated from the final frames of Tarkovsky's 'Stalker' . . . a mascot of the desolate, sky-crushed landscape of abandoned socialism, lured by exhaustion, boredom and this pervasive flatness.

For him, conversely, this train is a *fata morgana*, flashing out of and returning to nowhere. My life and the lives of my fellow travellers, as insubstantial as a feather of cirrus or a trace of smoke held slowly then exhaled, as slowly, from the lungs of the air. In these words, therefore, a confrontation occurs . . . between two nuances of nothing.

Bells Drowned in Air

I chased the doctor through stubble fields, as mud squelched over my boots. He had been prised from his pickling-jars of apricot brandy, decanted one litre at a time, by the sound of bells from the disused church—not heard from that direction in years. All alone in that desolate hamlet, he had put down his notebook and waddled, bearing his body-fat on guy-ropes of blood, too heavy and too indomitable to die. I cased him from a distance, conscious of crows.

The bell, just one of them in fact, was low-toned—it clanged as rain-clouds massed. I followed the doctor, director Tarr and the crew. I was in three places at once—my own, the director's, and the sad grey landscape I had scanned, at high speed, from trains on their way to Nyíregyháza or Békéscsaba. So it was that, mingled with the bell, I heard the jingle that was played to accompany station announcements, along with the rapid machine-gun fire of vowels and consonants from female announcers. But this faded and all I could hear, then, was the dreary tone of the bell.

The doctor reached the church, gasping for breath in over-used air like a washed-up whale. The sky, grown indolent in summer, had retained its rubbery thickness. It pressed him down and the bell, too, was strangely muffled—all the more so the closer he got. Pummelling space, it dived to the threshold of hearing.

In the bell-tower, perhaps ten metres above the ominous flatness of the *puszta*, a madman banged the bell with a stick. I stood beside the camera, watching the doctor as he watched the madman . . . but the madman took no notice, he kept on, saying over and over 'The Turks are coming! The Turks are coming!'. His eyes, that claimed the camera's focus, were as full moons eclipsed by solar shadow.

The doctor waddled back to his house where he boarded up the windows, decanted himself another litre of apricot brandy, then pickled his flesh against that horrible sound—to be found again in the spring, impossibly dead or alive. I took the madman's place and am banging that bell, in a space a hundred metres deep in the back of my head, as he strides out into the world each morning—as confident as a pasha, inspecting his captured lands.

Wide Roads in Sunlight

On a mural in Bartók tér, a frieze depicts this town's construction. One of the five pictures shows a commissar, directing what is portrayed as voluntary labour, against a backdrop of half-built apartment blocks— they are not yet clad in the beige and ochre stucco of the completed buildings. Similar efforts are taking place in towns and cities across Europe, ravaged by war, but this is different. This place is being built on fields, by a loess embankment overlooking a river, to house the proletariat of a heaven-storming steelworks itself the size of a town.

The town began life, in 1951, as Sztálinváros—Stalin City—and retained that name for several years. Then—as if to announce the era of 'all who are not against us are with us' in Secretary Kádár's words—it assumed the more neutral name of Dunaújváros, the new city on the Danube. The Socreal blocks, with their balconies and columns, were augmented by *panellak*, abstract statues, trees that had now grown from saplings to soften the landscape. The vision of a perfected, socialist world gave way to fifty-seven velvet varieties of Hobbesian struggle, as malls took their place in the suburbs and the steelworks, obsolete and worn, was broken up itself into light-industrial units.

What remains is still the past's idea of a future, yet neutralised by softer human concerns. I walk beside the wide road to the former steelworks, cudgelled by sunlight, wondering what it would be like to do so at the start of a twelve-hour shift with a labour camp at the back of one's mind. On the raised embankment, overlooking water-meadows that stretch for miles, I salute the statue of the helmeted, pickaxe-wielding workers who guard the Soviet horizon, as if they deserved that prominence in exchange for their sacrifice. I salute the past, as flawed as my own, without the self-righteousness that led to the exhumation of Kádár's remains. I think we can agree, I say to the statues, that the past is over and they silently share my joke.

Although from aerial photographs the impression is of a campus rather than a Hero City, there's heroism in the change. Prometheus himself might lie on a verge down there, beside an abstract statue of a sheet-metal moon or a sky-pointing, twisted needle of steel—no longer being eviscerated by an eagle but, instead, being gently teased by ants and midges in a post-historical meadow.

Spring

in memoriam Béla Bartók

Anxious foliage shivers. Scraping mud from boots, the setter of traps and sower of seeds is on the porch that faces at right-angles to the street. Night has arrived with its consignment of owls, and the empty stork's nest is backlit with stars. The glass's contents taste of trampled fire. In the clean room, shadows freeze but the main room is warm, its space hemmed in with dog-eared almanacs, jars and dishes.

Imagine a season like the fusion of all others, containing both burning sun and skin-removing, stuck-to-metal frost. Imagine being out there, in a village even gendarmes and preachers overlook. Imagine field upon field, all the way to the Verecke Pass. The sharp taste of *pálinka*, almost alkaline, flavoured with the slightest bouquet of apricots. Imagine a music purely exposed, nervous and restless and astringent, weaving in and out of this landscape like freight trains with Saharas of wheat. Imagine words that point at music, successfully and without embarrassment.

Soon, it's early morning and frost is polishing the gate, the fence, the tiles on the roof. Waking, cold and hungry, he puts on his woollen coat and the sound of a violin solo, rising as if out of a marsh, fills his mind with a delicate and diffident melancholy. Jupiter and Saturn wage conceptual war in the metal sky, as if it were midwinter, but it's March in 1881, the empire still stretches and the Emperor, whose wife is much more sympathetic, will settle down at lunchtime to his quickly-eaten *tafelspitz* and, as ever, conclude the day with an early night. March is all months. It contains a space, at dawn, in which the sun is poised on the orient horizon, from where the forebears came with their pentatonic scales, their language of slant-eyed vowels.

It is as possible for a peasant, in a low-key, single-street village like Balatonszentgyörgy or Rákoskeresztúr, to imagine himself hearing the fourth string quartet by a composer in the process of being born . . . to hum fragments out loud, with no capacity to write them down . . . as it is for a writer, in another land a century and twenty-five years later, to imagine him doing so. And every note and thought would flow from the purest spring, the spring of the all-possible.

A Bird in the Head

Yet again, I'm sitting at a table at the centre of Europe. It could be in a coffee house or an espresso bar, but today it's on the balcony of a five-storey bookshop. In front of me are the obligatory duo—espresso coffee and sparkling mineral water—along with a slice of *flodni*, layers of apple, walnut and poppy-seed divided by pastry. There is nowhere I need to be for several hours, no place that can't be visited later, or never again, or not at all.

So much happens that we need to resort, at times, to nothing, which is not (of course) the same as 'relaxing'—relaxing, as the adverts put it, is no more than consumption in the slow lane. This allows us to work through memories and experiences, purposelessly and in no predetermined order . . . crossing the thresholds of our lives in order to regard them more closely. Otherwise, it can all just vanish, moment buried under moment, none of it mattering at all as life just passes in a blur-stream of presence.

So, sipping mineral water and drinking sweet espresso, I recall the golden oriole I saw, a year ago, on the hill above Szekszárd. It was in bushes, about five metres away, and I thought it, at first, a painted bird, a toy of some kind, until it hopped into shadow. I had no idea that such a bird could appear so close to my own latitude . . . it seemed an alchemical creature made of sun-rays, able to fly as high as it liked without burning. I identified it on returning to England . . . in a book that told me that it was not as uncommon as I'd thought. But why would it be all the more miraculous for being rare?

How strange to sit in a Budapest bookshop, with a map of Hungary in my head as well as spread, on a one-to-one scale, around me . . . and how strange that, three hours to the south, there is a hill above a prosperous, wine-growing county town, on which a golden oriole appeared, one year ago, for a matter of moments. Somewhere between that present and this, my consciousness widens and I feel—deluded as this may be—as if there is a space that is safe from time.

Midnight at the Hotel Savaria

It's as if the hotel's been built for my benefit. At the end of September, in midweek, the tourist season is certainly over—even Austrians with toothache are avoiding Szombathely, a city of Roman remains and cut-price dentists.

So, after my evening meal—at the bright, refurbished modern hotel down the road that I would have stayed in if I'd not come here first, and impulsively booked—I settle down in my pre-war room. Not properly heated, with a rickety chair. With oversized wardrobes and a bed with the suspension of a harpsichord. With a TV that hints at sixty-four channels but reveals only four—one shows a concert featuring Bartók's *Dance Suite*, but when that ends I'm down to three, two of which appear to be showing the same bicycle race. So I switch it off, at eleven o'clock, and insert myself into paper-thin sheets.

Then I write myself a letter from here to there to here, from my present self on behalf of my past self to my present self—conscious of the six-and-a-half years that have passed, but recalling the cold and hearing the creak of the door as, having put on my shirt and jeans, and having removed my wallet from beneath the pillow to pocket it in case of unlikely theft, I lock the door behind me and walk down the corridor. My room isn't en-suite and I have to turn left, as the clock strikes midnight, to find the toilets—where, I note, there are more urinals than cubicles, the relic of a collectivist era of boozy delegations.

The silence in the corridors implies that I am the only guest, and the strangeness of my being here doubles the length of my slash. And, from the other side of my time-stretched self, it is as if I could walk into those toilets, tap myself on the shoulder in the dead of that night, and re-assure me-him that I am still alive and writing on my-his, as well as my-my, behalf. I would, of course, omit the precise details of what will follow that night, those years of continuous, half-grasped presents. I would also attempt—and fail—to pit this feat against my own mortality, but the act of reaching back seems defiant enough.

As long as I live, I will always be a guest at the Hotel Savaria. Closing my eyes, I can feel myself falling—back, and back to my silence in that place, through days and years that are shed like peel.

Two O'clock

At two o'clock, the native English speaker at the Török Ignác Gymnasium retires to the Sulyán. He acknowledges the students queuing for ice creams and orders, in his improving yet imperfect Hungarian—a milky coffee and a cherry strudel are promptly delivered.

Outside, the citizens of Gödöllő, a commuter town to the east of Budapest, go about their business . . . by now, he can recognise a number of faces, from teachers and parents to plumbers and electricians who've serviced his flat. He will go home to cook, read and listen to music, phone his girlfriend down the track in the *sinful city* and, if the sunshine lasts, may take a walk through the park, past the renovated palace where Queen Sissi moped. On other nights, there'll be films or plays at the Petőfi Cultural Centre. The strudel is, as ever, delicious.

I'm an Englishman at the end of a holiday. It's a pristine afternoon in April and I've three hours before the bus. I'll visit the town museum again, risk being taken under the wing of a volunteer who'll practice her rusty German on me . . . eat a pizza by the station before staring, from the bus, at the backs of statues in Heroes' Square as I re-enter the city. In a couple of days I'll be reviewing my snapshots, two thousand kilometres to the west.

We both eat cherry strudel and drink milky coffee. The tables are the same. Our faces are only slightly different. Each of us is as a ghost to the other. We are almost alike but can only stare . . . communication resides in this two-way mirror that's invisible to other customers. Each of us embodies a choice, but only one of us can write this account. It's as if we're here to take part in a silent duel, to see who will do so . . . the first who leaves will possess the burden of choice and the solace of narrative.

It has to be me. But, if I return to Gödöllő he'll still be there, like Joyce at his table in the Istrian town of Pula, expressing what I missed but missing what I express.

A Foreign Field

You're far too small, like the rest of us, to appear on a map—but I can take down this atlas and, in an orange square at the right-hand edge of Page 87, I can envisage you sleeping, the occupant of one of at least a hundred flats in the block. Cars grumble past on the main road out of the city, the one shown in yellow—the final suburban trains are leaving, on the deep green line that heads to Page 88 and beyond, and a drunk without a ticket fumbles in vain.

In Rákosfalva—the 'village of the Serbs'—a hundred thousand citizens will have settled down, in eleven-storey tower-blocks raised in the Seventies. Some will be asleep, preparing themselves for the early starts of your adopted land. Others will be awake, listening to traffic and the soft roar of a plane as it curls into Ferihegy.

As I look at the map, a shadowy place appears. I picture the trolley buses, so frequent that they move in convoy during the rush-hour—the old people's home and the crèche beside it, the shabby bar called 'the Spur' where workers drink bottled beer at seven in the morning. I see the kiosks outside the mall, the store in the corrugated precinct where I queue for small things we've forgotten to buy.

Then other vistas appear, and a confusion of streets entices me to wander. I find myself in two places at once or cross, in an instant, from one municipality to another as my memory wanders at the speed of light. But I return, exhausted, in a matter of seconds to the room in which you sleep.

Your body's so close that I can feel the texture of your hair as I type. But the atlas, for me, is where you are now—that orange square's the corridor through which we connect. I am here and t/here and alone-and-with-you, surveying a foreign field in which you rest and I, unreasonably, persist in my absence.

So I replace the atlas on the shelf, as if it were possible to close this city — but as my meditation comes to a close, the connection persists. I know that I am inscribed, invisibly, in streets we have come to know so well . . . and that I will not leave them, again, until both of us have died. And I knew it would end like this—in the space between the atlas on the shelf, and the one that persists in my head.

VI

Blue Skin

Magdalenefjord

I build myself a shelter and await the world's end, surrounded by the blue skin of the far north.

Whalers' graves, coughed up by permafrost's heave, are exposed on the peninsula at Gravneset. The cruise ships have gone. Blubber ovens are encased in geodes of frost.

Attendants have removed the litter left by garrulous parties. No-one saw me sneak onto land—no-one saw me build my cabin. The police hut closes for the winter, the patrol boat sails off. I'm left with six month's supplies of thin Norse air and, so far to the south as to seem equatorial, my family, friends and colleagues discuss my absence (I hope).

Terns, barnacle geese and eider ducks have flown south. The sky's a hail-sack. Compass needles of Polar night are about to strike. Their syringes contain a cocktail of blues, a serum that will seal me into an extinguished planet's sleep.

And I await the world's end. Or spring. Every day, the sun grows weaker and, each night, the star-dunes scintillate more brightly. I am both in deep space and on the naked face of the earth.

Comfortless Cove

The air is so clear that I can smell my own breath.

I walk the headland on a clear November day, under the light of a moon that edits out the sun. I walk beside a woman even paler than you, although her hair is as black as yours is blonde. I am sure that I have breathed her from me and, when I address her, she responds with an echo of my own voice.

If we made love—which is semantically possible—we might people this expanse with blue-skinned ghost-children. Their hearts would be as ultramarine as these hills. Emanations, echoes . . . and so the Arctic's first great city would form.

Siberian driftwood lies on the strand, the spines of giants whose mush-flesh sags in ice on water turning to ice. I try to listen to what it says—its shamanic narratives might offer the hope of cosmic order. Which one is the World-Tree? The world is always its own aftermath and its own negation.

My night-haired companion disappears as the moon sets. I believe the sun stirred itself for half an hour or so, a blind man brandishing a torch in a room already lit.

Motivation

I am not here, I decide, for the world's end after all. I am here for the spring that follows. I am here for the test of confidence, the promise of blue sky.

If the strategy fails, I will be found beneath a pyramid of snow one morning in my home town bed. Still naked, as I prefer to sleep, but as pale as marble.

'Refinement, subtlety and silence' (according to Kenneth Grant) are the keys to magickal success. I no longer practice magick. I have no desire to become a magus. But I am thinking myself into a magickal space, that cools and tempers me in all ways. And yes, it is a means of escape from coarseness, unsubtlety and noise.

I am here as I write and I am equally there. I am as stretched, as ever, on latitude and longitude and my vigil is too luxurious to dissuade me. To be here, awake, at midnight, the stove still warm—a clot of imagined laudanum in my throat, the scent of a single candle in my lungs.

Only you, who are too far away, could hope to tempt me from this.

Forget-Me-Nots

Candles of *aufeis* form in front of glaciers. I stand before them, as faint light billows like a poppy. I count the days until spring. I count the days of my life.

My memory is too precise. I can think to myself that, on such and such a day in such and such a year, I was *here* and did *this*. Life becomes a heap of scree, each fragment catalogued. In thirty thousand days, a biography forms like ice around the new-born fallen to earth.

So far to the south that I can only touch you with my breath, you walk from the metro in a gathering fog and vendors watch you from their spread-out cloths.

To the north of me there is sea-ice, to the north of the North Pole there is only sky—black as a hole in space, a tunnel to no time where my small, besieged identity is of no concern.

I wish you the light from Vega and Altair, to pluck with your eyes when fog abates. Perhaps this is what I will remember, above all, from this day—a memory of faraway stars, and not so faraway you.

Drifting Snow, across the Screen

Night starts here, as I open this file and replace the whiteness of the lands outside with the whiteness of this screen. These words are night's emissaries.

Outside, the polar demons are mine to deploy as I please. The vast cold silent spaces of Svalbard are as far from human parlance as the surface of Sedna—the plutoid named for an Arctic goddess of the depths.

After man, the rats will grow enormous and fierce and hunt rabbits the size of antelopes on revived savannahs. If any polar bears remain, they will hunt in the depths with fins and scales and evolve into snow-coloured sharks. This is what it said in a book I bought for my father, twenty-five years ago when the threat seemed tenuous. Now, I cannot tell what I will return to.

Like the narrator of M.P. Shiel's *The Purple Cloud*, I could come to be the only one left, at least in theory, but there is no desire in me to destroy. If I curate the ruins of the world for the rest of my life, it will be a life worth living in the eye of the blind Creatrix.

Perhaps, already, a howl is all that remains, a howl that I ventriloquise. Then why am I so calm? I wonder, propped on the pillow of what Is.

Aurora Borealis

The pelt of snow-covered day. The negative pelt of polar night, dusted with a flurry of stars, intermittently stained with the flowing lights of the Aurora.

From here to the Pole, no voices. Cold creeps in, clamping bones, through thick wooden walls. The faint gold light from my window is the lantern of a boat on a sea the size of a cosmos.

In all directions, there is infinite frost and silence and the skin of my former lovers is crumbling on my hands. I could shatter like glass and these words would disperse, each letter as present yet as insubstantial as a midge.

Outside—donning layer upon layer of synthetic furs, I open the double-layered doors—the delicate greens and ambers flare in shaft-deep dark, a witch-dance plasma I can only touch with my eyes. And, even then, after thirty seconds or so the lashes begin to thicken, each with a scabbard of ice of its own.

There is a moment after the final moment, the epilogue of time—I've wanted to reach into that moment for O so long but, having found it, I'm emptier than ever before.

Infinite Wind

The wind is blue. The wind conveys the end of the world. The wind is the unified voice of stars. The wind divides me from my species. Miles of frozen, freezing, frigid water sings to the baton of the wind.

The sheer blue god of nowhere and nothing looms as I bow down standing straight.

Extinction of self and species, the blindness of an eye that is utterly blue without medicinal white . . . these face me in a mirror hewn by a hurricane's axe.

In blizzard I may sleep, a Neolithic tribesman curled in a burial chamber's egg. Or perhaps I shall stretch beside you, lord to your lady, as if on a raised tomb in a Minster of ice. Queen of all that I can claim as my kingdom, in death as in life.

As I lie in my bed, the blue wind moans. I am thinking myself south then recoiling north, a Viking from an uninhabitable land. Only the wind connects.

Weather Report

There are rusted implements in geological time, including metal cans that are marked with swastikas.

They came to Krossfjorden to chart the weather, here at the nearest point to the hole in the Earth where, in their febrile narratives, the blonde beasts emerged. There was no mitochondrial DNA back then to connect the Aryans to the Semites and the San, to bury the lie that we are not all Africans in exile.

The purest air in Europe settled their lungs. On the scree-laden shore, they strutted like Aesir. Now, they come into focus as I clench my eyes—freezing in greatcoats, watching every word of their banter.

No thunderstorms here, to burst, Wagnerian. Only delicate washes of sun. Then wind, frost, cudgels of hail. Head-foot shivers. Tents, half-buried in blue-tinged drift.

I want to tell them that the war is over, but they are much too old for me to talk to. Their children roam the byways of my locale, in docile raiding parties that appear each summer. There is no longer a hole in the Polar ice for overmen to step through—just a hole in the sky through which the 'purple legions' of cosmic indifference advance.

On the Brilliance of Lichen

Green, black, orange . . . clinging on, in unawareness. No negotiation's possible with such life-forms—older than we will ever be, more passive and resigned than our corpses.

There are experts who can name each species. I can only extol the beauty of their negation, as I circle a place where language turns to a yawn of millions of years.

When my words are gone, and my ashes have been dispersed or my frozen body mummified to another genus of rock, there will still be lichen. There was lichen at the beginning of land, there will be lichen at its end. It is immune to glory and boredom alike (we guess). We can only conduct a dialogue with its being-in-the-world, its exquisite colourful blank.

Apes let loose, we swarm from forests and clamber over the rocks of the earth, beneath unanswering stars and the ghost of a wise old naked father ape in the sky . . . or, if we are wiser, a fair young maiden ape arched naked from east to west. Or—if we are wiser still—beneath the unanswering stars.

Lichen outstays our welcome. Is naming it enough? We offer it our many languages, then fall silent in what seems to it like no time at all.

Ursus Maritimus

Our enemy, in so far as it is curious, can run at thirty kilometres an hour, and can kill a seal with a blow of its claw.

Our enemy when it is hungry and harassed, when it misunderstands our body-language.

Our enemy, because it lives on meat like almost everything of any size in these parts. Like us.

Our enemy, a soldier blessed with a built-in body-arsenal, who will not apologise or atone but move on to the next feast. Intelligent, yes, but beyond anthropomorphism.

Our enemy, ripping up a badly-equipped researcher on an ice-floe in view of his colleagues. Red scraps remaining. Or a teenage girl on the hills above Longyearben.

Our enemy, sharing the same blue planet.

Our enemy—marooned, starving, on an ice-floe drifting out into the mildness of an Arctic summer noon, too exhausted to swim to safety. Lost from sight—like so many of our enemies, our neighbours and our friends.

Cabin Fever

Ghosts propagate. In swarming dark, the names and faces of my biography are challenged, assailed and devoured by those from Beyond. I no longer know, for certain, who I was and the strategy that brought me here is a wand's wave. I am alone . . . on an ice-floe, an asteroid, a thermal or the beard of God.

You take so many forms. Your shape mutates with the colour of your hair. You speak to seduce me in all languages. My sex is raised on invisible girders. All the flowers of the north repeat themselves on my throat.

I am trapped in the moment after the moment in which I am located, constantly one step ahead and the footprints I have left are filled with snow. I do not know if I will leave this cabin ever again, or if I will see another living creature that is not my projection. And what am I—a projection of ice? A shadow cast by void?

You stroke my chest as if in reassurance, ghost propositioning ghost. There is white-out inside these walls as well as outside. My name is white on white. I could be you and I could be the ground beneath the ground, I could be dead and, no less, the mirror of death—a transparent man through which the whiteness studies itself.

Distance of Spring

The clock has frozen. Crystals of time-frost clog its interior, no matter how fierce the heat from the stove.

In circumpolar night, I lose track. I measure the passage of time by the books I try to read and the number of words with which I nourish the keyboard.

It is too late and too early to go out. The tern, that bomber of heads, is soaking up light at the other pole. Mother bears feed cubs with a rich thick milk in the ground. I am stored here, counting the floaters in my eyes.

Spring here means fiercer storms, then the briefest blossoming. Light that hovers, rimming horizons. The shouts of cruise-passengers, experiencing the affordable Arctic. Salubrious air with hardly a hint of pollen.

Spring will record my emergence. It will expel my words that are the product of its absence, dark blocks of despair and resolution.

But the stars, for now, can offer no time to the clock's crevasse. I exist in the space between their searchlights.

The Books I Read in My Sleep

I turn over in bed . . . and the books are all replaced by the dream-books of my sleep. I must have written them without knowing that I had done so, in such a frenzy of inspiration that they published themselves. I look across, with bleary eyes, at my traveller's ice-floe library—those snowfield editions that only exist Up Here.

THE BOOK OF ICE-FLOES. THE BOOK OF THE PURIFIED MIND. THE BOOK OF FROZEN MEAT. THE BOOK OF WHITE CLOUD. THE SVALBARD BOOK OF THE UNBURIED. THE HEAVY BOOK. THE BOOK OF PEMMICAN. THE BOOK OF ABSOLUTE NORTH. THE BOOK OF VIRGINITY REGAINED. THE BOOK THE POLAR BEAR HAS READ. THE BOOK OF WHITE STONES AND WOODEN CROSSES. THE WHALEBONE BOOK. THE BOOK OF THE CONQUEST OF THE LOMONOSOV RIDGE. THE BOOK OF LOST MONKS AND VIKINGS BLOWN OFF COURSE. THE BOOK I WANTED YOU TO READ BUT NEVER DARED TO ASK. THE TRUTH BOOK. THE SERUM BOOK. THE BOOK KICKED ABOUT IN THE ICE. THE BOOK OF CRACKED BELLS AND FROZEN CANDLES. THE DEATH BOOK. THE JESTING BOOK. THE BOOK THAT HIDES IN THE SHADOWS CAST BY LICHEN. THE BOOK YOU WILL NOT READ BECAUSE I FORGOT TO ASK

and their titles swim before my bleary, night-encrusted eyes as I turn over and over and over again in the precarious warmth of my bed.

The Globe Shrunk Tight

Burrowed in aurora-riven sleep, I dream of orchards laden with fruit and of the songs of thrushes bubbling from dawn to dusk. I dream of swifts that scatter themselves in early summer breezes. I dream of mornings when the sun floods in like a tide of molten gold, and I dream I erase these things with an eraser of solid ice.

Surrounded by zero pulse, I wake and count the days of my vigil to come. There is no life between this bed and the disdainful stars. Light years of silence weight my tongue. You appear to me in a loose white dress—the menstrual trickle down your thigh is freezing as you turn to the south.

Her pale head heavy as metal, I read aloud. Tempted here by the promise of purity, I find that I cannot speak to call you back. It is as if my language froze the very first time I breathed, into the northerly airflow that metallic autumn night, as the crystals of my words fell tinkling to earth. Where they fell, I fondly convince myself, there will be flowers in spring . . . or the very first saprophytes to feed on these shores.

A Saturnine Moon

I put on my second skin and stagger outside. My breath shimmers and tinkles, the water-vapour freezing as it touches the night.

The green scythe of a saturnine moon is barely over the horizon. It makes the sky bleed but blood freezes, as if beneath my hands or the earth.

I want to erase this night and return to the south. I am tired of this purity—I would smile at the sight of a fly, and dance if a wasp flew into my gloves.

But, wherever we are, we exist at the edge of stone and metal. Our vitality is circumscribed and, in mapping all the death and indifference that surrounds our narrow nexus of life, we take on something of that death and it hardens in our souls like a pearl. It is one of the ways we learn to die.

That moon is the gesture of its own unending death, and this brings it to life. I watch it disappear, as star-flocks move across the ebony pastures of night.

It shines like a key, a key I could hold in my hands. Its indifference reconciles me to my own indifference. Its love is the love of the scalpel for the corpse.

Itinerant

And then, in a dream, I walk through dense green forests and relish the coolness of moss. I am near, I sense, to the Pacific. The ocean widens my lungs. You are out of sight yet tangible at the tips of my fingers.

Beyond the ordeals of ice, there is a far-off land where all is hushed but nothing is chilled. In walking towards you I am following the Tao, the Tao I lost when young and have escaped, twice over, to find. I wanted silence and simplicity and a deeper sense of being alive. Sleep is the gateway. I risk red berries from a branch at the height of my mouth.

Moss-green, berry-red and bird's egg-blue . . . the sky's impersonal cathedral, leaves and fruit in the aisles, the rustle of your feet or are they wings and the deft movements of a deer in the thicket to my left . . . I am homing in on another kind of death, in which I do not crumple or come apart or seep from my wounds but turn, instead, to an Other. A man of Tao, blown clean by the breeze that authors his cells, no longer anxious and ambitious and absurd.

What a dream! I think as I wake to the dark, the walls and the steel-veined cold outside. It offers a place beyond this place that only this place could have led to—the shortest route via the Pole, as is so often the case.

Impossible Music

Chords succeed each other like flowers on a mountain path. They choreograph my solitude and point to passages un-reached, and archipelagos that are mine to name but never to conquer.

I am so far from you here that I permit the music to define you. The music shimmers as if in space not time, and its white leaves continue to fall like rain.

You retreat, in a procession of former selves stretching all the way back to our very first meeting, and beyond to a day when I would have walked past you in the town in which we lived without knowing or even suspecting what you would mean to me. Perhaps I first saw you on holiday as a child, not knowing and not knowing my unknowing.

I think of your existence before I was born, in wordless infancy. I think of the cadence, fifty years of our rise and fall.

And here you are, and are not. I am lonely and I miss you, that much is clear to the point of banality. I retreat beyond you, only to find you again, and I find you here in your absence as it hollows a space around this music.

The Grave of the Mariner

Bleaching bones on a bed of black moss. A coffin, prised open by wind and assaults of ice. No mummified skin to stun the attention. This is the *memento mori* I seek, a skull picked clean of its origins and labels.

This land's indifference can contain no mariner's homily, no attentive wedding-guest or kirk on a low green hill. Its stories end in petrified gestures, in sockets too cold for crows to peck.

The pitilessness in the bear's eye reduces us to the distractions of meat. The bears should be writing this narrative, with scraps of my carcass they inscribe on snow. The bears whose ancestors might have licked the skull of the mariner clean.

I can humanise nothing here, not even myself. These iron processes extend from the birth of stars to their heat-death and the final, following cold of which they are heralds.

I inspect the open coffin, a void un-named by a void.

After Such a Long Repose

The first dream is made entirely of the petals of roses, arranged into the semblance of a world. Even the meat of our bodies and the bricks of our houses are fragrant, faintly leathery, and scatter at a touch to invented winds.

The second dream is made entirely of Oriental sweetmeats: halvah, baklava, Turkish delight. I bite into the walls of palaces and nibble the slightly salty, almond-tasting curves of your flesh. I am a mouth without a voice, a hungry yet solicitous mouth.

The third dream is of spices. The fourth, of jewels. The fifth, of citrus fruit. The sixth, of truffles nudged into view and smelling of sex and the embalming earth.

The seventh dream is of ice and I wake, rubbing invisible ice from my eyes, to walk to the window and observe the newly-risen sun. The possibilities have re-ignited and I long, as never before, to be out of this Calvinist place, to forget these austerities forever.

But, in scarcely an hour, I embrace their peace once more and, sitting back as if with a draught of laudanum in my hand, I think of the placid sleep of the explorers, the silence stretched from here to the galactic rim . . . and the permanent shrug on the shoulders of the dead.

The Sleeping Knights

The sleep ahead of me, whose nature I can only guess at, teases me when I fall from the cliff and forget that I was ever me, forget that I was ever looked at or loved or had a name or walked the streets of an ever-expanding map.

Heroes under ice are dreaming these words and the breath that blossoms from my mouth is theirs. They sleep and wait, without knowing that they sleep or wait, for spring to come and, as they sleep, their flesh repeats itself in snowdrop after snowdrop.

The kindness of the embalmer makes them smile. Ages pass and they continue to dream in the aftermath of dream, dreaming the world of which they are no longer a part but which regards them, through a prism of admiration and fear, as the psychonauts of the Aeon to come, the name-shedding prophets of a nameless fate.

I love them and I shun them. I think of them, at the far side of the world, under their skis as the faint accretions of snow continue year on year. Pure being, cooler and more distant than the moon and terrifyingly beautiful . . . lodged in an afterworld I grasp with blind nocturnal hands.

It Seems a Pity

To create a text that resides in the aftermath of text . . . to leap like a diver from the end of one's final sentence on earth, leaving the work complete as blue skin freezes over one's splash.

Words that express the absence of words, that sum up the universe by being vacant—posthumous, random marks on Palaeozoic stone.

Our frozen bodies the found poems of another age, something to mark with a cross or whatever sacred symbol's in vogue.

I accepted this commission only to be bored, after the first fascination, by blues and whites and greys and the creaks from all around and the gobsmacking tedium of 'whirling drift'.

The hope was to sculpt that mineral resource, carefully, over the course of a polar winter and return to spring with an iceberg under each arm. How ridiculous to think I could cope, that I would not miss the warmth and the noise and the crush of bodies in the end.

I must leave this silence and this cold to the genuine saints.

I Wake to Bare Rock

Waking from a delicate and gentle sleep, I notice that the air has warmed and that the ice on the window has melted.

Outside, there is bare rock and the bone of a whale spreads out like a fan. The first cruise party of the summer is coming ashore. The sun is out and creeps from hour to hour around the horizon.

I gather up my notes and board the ship without receiving a second glance, despite the fact that, when I see myself reflected, both my face and hands are deeply blue. Self-conscious in my blueness, I squat in an empty cabin and, in days, am back in England with my blue tan fading. Once more, the idea of the Arctic is lodged at the back of my mind, in a place I can return to by sitting quietly.

Ice continues to melt and currents shift. The mineral resources at the Pole are charted and competing claims are heard. Sea-levels rise and the ice that locked me in appears, unfrozen, in flooded tropical harbours. A polar bear carcass slowly dissolves to its constituent atoms and we drink it, unthinkingly, with an alabaster snarl.

But still, the hermetic blues of the Arctic hover, as ever, at the edge of our sight. We affirm them through escape.

VII

from *Departures*

The Remains

I walked through valleys of broken china. On either side, smashed cups and plates lay under the evening sky, white as a ransacked ossuary, in the Longport doldrums.

Villages, once blurred by smoke from beehives of brick, infested a tangled map. As I walked, the terraces appeared to shrink to my height. Samosas and oatcakes slept in corner shops. Slag, grassed over, offered perspectives on a mottled geography—beyond, in stoat-grey hills, the moon lay in wait.

I proceeded from town to town, along charcoal canals and under motorways, past smashed-faced warehouses and drive-in restaurants, pursuing his ligatured ghost. His hollow eyes and body-jerk had already been conveyed to the sky in smoke, his music consigned to tribute and requiem.

I was twenty, full of unrequited lust and megalomania but a lively person to have around (no doubt). From the far south-west, I bore my accent like a sunhat into the glowering regions of (post-) industrial (post-) travail.

In the next ten years, I visited football ground after football ground—only the shape of the stands varied, it was all one game—pretending to be a homeboy when the home team scored, a benevolent neutral when they didn't. I sat in a hundred pubs with my old mate Chris, drank three or four pints of mild or bitter for lunch—at the afternoon's end, there were heroic messy journeys, on spontaneous trains with walk-on long-distance Cheap Day Returns, fortified by chips and the algebras of Green 'Uns and Pinks.

In the end, that collage of a mini-conurbation stands out. Not the home of my psychopomp, for that was (comparatively) well-heeled Macclesfield. Instead, when I recall the worked-out lands of my twenties I find myself most often in Cobridge, Burslem or Fenton—those Interzones of red brick and rust.

On my final visit to Vale Park, in 1988, the inevitable happened at last—after forty minutes, fog descended and at half-time it enveloped the ground. They even played 'Didn't We Have It All?' by Whitney Houston in an effort to repel it—but in vain. This is where it began to end . . . an experiment in assumed identity that sees me back here, in the sodden Hesperides, and the singer touched from a distance on celluloid.

D.S. in Köln

Halfway across a difficult world, I was immersed in a strangeness that froze my journey. Peacock buildings bloomed and the sound of my busking died in a pigeon paperhouse. I ate a mixed fruit slice and gulped down coffee from a plastic cup as I paused—my sleepless eyes wedged open, my veins full of wasp-fur, I laid in wait for bankers and tourists.

And hunger stalked me from the shadows, as I lived on snacks and the beery air of the West. And hearing only moon, I sang to amuse the sun.

I was rescued by men in leather coats who took me to their castle, tuned up their instruments, positioned their tapes and encouraged me to sing whatever came into my throat. Suddenly, I was an Artist, freeing words from their cages for several hours at a time. I sent home records by registered post and received solicitous responses, in a language whose nuances I was beginning to unlearn.

Now, I order in German, sing in broken English and dream in Japanese and moon-speak. I still don't understand what I'm trying to express and this keeps me awake. I can't recall sleeping for at least five years and my lovers don't explain, irrational mistresses all with enormous hips. In this wealthy, rebuilt city of galleries and cake-shops, I intrude—a cloud-headed shaman—from a monstrous narrative, brought here by the Great God Dromomania.

And at the end of a world-long journey, even my flesh seems vivid and strange, as mad as the hair that mumbles into my eyes.

'Bring me coffee or tea' I say to the attentive groupie, feeding live fish in the carp-pond of my mouth. From now on, too, I'll be a stranger to myself—looking in, from the depths, at my diving-suited likeness. So green my face, as it struggles for breath but stays alive—my voice not mine, but something I fell into like a groove that encircles the earth.

So beware, sad moon! I am singing myself to sleep, but it will take a lifetime.

Audition for the Part of a God

for Scott Walker

He even hid in a monastery to escape the sight of himself seen face-on, under spotlights—to escape the sound of himself revised and reinforced by an adoring choir.

How strange it must have been to sing his torch songs to millions on a Saturday night of stale bacon suppers, wedged between game shows and the latest black-and-white soccer action. No-one could have understood this fully, but he lent those evenings a semi-Bohemian momentum—a sense that excitement was in reach, for even the comfortable and the infirm, in a limitless and ecstatic decade.

But later, he chased songs through drizzly streets, another man that everybody wanted to meet but nobody wanted to hire. Pursued by his former self, an Apollo from whom clothing was torn in an ironic rendition of the legend of Marsyas. When off-guard, he might catch his face in the vinyl dumps of record stores, awaiting its reduction to the scale of a CD cover.

He hid in one monastery after another. Looking into the mirror is hard. Confronting the image of oneself, in the market-place of popular culture, is an existence of permanent embarrassment in the face of a being of rumour and myth that shares one's name.

So he decided to audition for a final role, that of *deus absconditus*. That way, he'd be as invisible as he could hope to become—more so, perhaps, than if he'd simply altered his name and face—in the best of all worlds, which combined the artistic freedom of non-recognition with a steady income from artistic success.

You might say that he *came through*. He can wait there for songs—or, at least, for cryptic words and compatible sonic textures—burying his head in the ellipses of the avant-garde.

You could choose to celebrate his choice, his refusal to play the role of the aging pop-star. If you were really kind, you would leave a whisky bottle, filled with ice-cool spring water from the Vaucluse or Auvergne, outside the door of his house.

The Drowning Coast

for WG Sebald and Brian Eno

A resumption of bells, heard through storm water. Out there, Holland-ward, in a stout-brown sea, to the right of the Sole Bay flotillas. And a dribble of bones, in a cliff-face permanent as talc.

After the lost day, the indifferent night. The church, slow-fallen from the sand rise, makes bass-profound music. At the same time, inland, the photographs of its skeleton fade, fall from another cliff with the bones of their decipherers.

A misty, ragged rain sets in and muffles the bells, turns water to pitch. The city sleeps and its memories, already long-illegible, are pawed from encrusted surfaces. To the north, the village with its single street bears the name that it slid from.

I envisage a hysterical Victorian poet with an oversized mane of auburn hair, pacing the cliff path long since crumbled, contemplating shingle and intoning lines of extravagant, redundant musicality. He exhausted himself and died, no more alive than the God he had arraigned or the burghers exhumed by the sea's claws.

The sun, once risen here, is as if *on fire* to leave. And the sea forgets what it eats—fragments without price, unintelligible merchandise. It still encroaches, threatening the remains . . . the symbol of that which threatens the eyes.

All washed over, bells ground down to sand, forever lost and forgotten say the comforters, removing regrets and hopes. They pull the sea, like a blanket of night—no moon no stars—through the holes of our eyes, dislodging silver coins. The drowning men and the drowning city, ordained and damned, provide an answer to the Revenue's lanterns.

What I Wanted to Say about György Ligeti

The dematerialisation's as immense as ever—geographies of sound diffuse into cirrus patterns seen from an aircraft at midday. Solaris illusions fool me into seeing what I loved and has passed forever, cities and clocktowers and trees that wave in parks and cyclists moving under them as pigeons and starlings scatter.

All of this is melting, steaming, forming and un-forming and the colours that reflect this mingling are unearthly, eerie, as delicate as those in a nebula, firework colours out of Stravinsky made still more ethereal and extreme . . . so tenuous in their evasion of mind and tongue, in a world of ceaseless and hyperactive change where clocks become clouds and clouds are sugar watches melting in sun, everything resisting the solidity that is death.

You wove all this, candyfloss flavoured with the dark blood of your sombre heritage, the pain of a clown's there if we look for it and you laid it down lightly, your lost Erdély, slow carts trundling between bare hills, ramshackle villages with long main streets, manic dances and yellow stars in the air.

In protean transformations from the grave to the sky, your music lent itself so perfectly to the acid overdrive of the spaceman's escape and its chromo-delirium. You spent your life in take-off, winging from difficult roots as, that autumn week in 1956, you escaped the institute, the imprisoned country and crossed a continent to sleep, for days, on arrival as if in pupation. You evaded the trap of what you would have been, a caterpillar in a tomb of thick glass, a professor growing old in a mellowing city, to deal firsthand and on equal terms with the Tao.

Your brain has become anonymous dust but we can listen and dream with your thoughts and, each birthday, sharing yours I can't help but try to resurrect you. Looking at clouds in a late spring sky, I can hear the infinite droplets of your music. And all notes remain possible—even the *classical* remains as everything warms, expands, grows strange and mobile in the quickening world.

Dreams of the Caucasus

The landscapes we unroll from ourselves, in dreams or in daydreams, can tease with imprecision—scrunching the maps we make with our own, somnambulistic hands. And so it is with virtual landscapes made of text, and thought, and spaces between the fingers of thought. Imagination enters the gaps, with absurd and sometimes miraculous results.

In Herzog's film, the foundling Kaspar Hauser announces that he has 'dreamt of the Caucasus', as he struggles to relate his dreams for the very first time. Yet the 'Caucasus' he describes has absolutely nothing of that war-torn, sabre-dance-and-pomegranate landscape about it—it's the tidy landscape of a train-set, surveyed on flickering film. Reached out for, in sleep, by a wise and humble fool.

Each day, these days, we visit more places than we can name or catalogue. This applies, however grounded we are. We move between countries, continents and worlds and are besieged, at every point, by locations we have either ceased to occupy or have never visited. Shuffling maps like Tarot, we learn by comparison and contrast . . . never in one place only. Not even I in this one, this city that has been a home, of sorts, for much of my life. All becomes dream, the dream of a single place with infinite roads.

Like Kaspar, I will exit my life with an Earth in my head that is very sparingly spotlit. Trying to extend myself towards the darker regions, unsure if I've even been living on a spherical planet, I am nonetheless reaching and striving, wanting to be its citizen and wearing the world, upon my shoulders, as lightly as I wear my head. And this leads me into a shadowy world, an egg made of wind and perfume and light, that struggles to break across these pages.

So—when life concludes—what was real and what was dreamt?

Here lie monsters. Here lie humans. But encounter is all.

www.ingramcontent.com/pod-product-compliance
Lightning Source LLC
Chambersburg PA
CBHW022157080426
42734CB00006B/480